Accounting Systems and Controls

Tutorial

Sheriden Amos

Michael Fardon

Published by Osborne Books Limited
Tel 01905 748071
Email books@osbornebooks.co.uk
Website www.osbornebooks.co.uk

Design by Laura Ingham

Printed by CPI Group (UK) Limited, Croydon, CRO 4YY, on environmentally friendly, acid-free paper from managed forests.

British Library Cataloguing in Publication Data
A catalogue record for this book is available from the British Library

ISBN 978 1909173 910

Contents

Introduction

Qualifications covered

This book has been written specifically to cover the Unit 'Accounting Systems and Controls' which is mandatory for the following qualifications:

AAT Professional Diploma in Accounting – Level 4
AAT Professional Diploma in Accounting at SCQF – Level 8

This book is an Osborne Books AAT Tutorial book for material only tested by the Professional Level Synoptic Assessment. The Synoptic Assessment also includes elements of:

- Management Accounting: Budgeting
- Management Accounting: Decision and Control
- Financial Statements of Limited Companies

These subjects are covered in the relevant Osborne Books AAT Tutorials.

The synoptic assessment is a computer based assessment, based around a business. Pre-release material is available to you ahead of the assessment. This can be studied to encourage you to think about the areas the synoptic assessment covers and how they interact.

This book specifically covers:

- the roles and responsibilities of the accounting function within an organisation, including legislation and regulations
- evaluating effectiveness of the organisation's accounting system and procedures and the internal controls within them, particularly looking at fraud, ethics and sustainability
- recommendations to improve the organisation's accounting system and how this will affect the staff within the organisation

Osborne Study and Revision Materials

Our materials are tailored to the needs of students studying this unit and revising for the assessment. They include:

- **Student Zone:** access to Osborne Books online resources
- **Osborne Books App:** Osborne Books ebooks for mobiles and tablets

Visit www.osbornebooks.co.uk for details of study and revision resources and access to online material.

1 Introduction to accounting systems and controls

this chapter covers...

This first chapter is an introduction to the Unit 'Accounting Systems and Controls.'

The chapter will explain:

- *the reasons why this Unit is rather different from any other you will have encountered so far in your studies*
- *how this Unit relates to the synoptic assessment*
- *how to deal with the synoptic assessment*
- *what will be expected of you as you complete the Unit*
- *how to organise your method of working to make the most of your resources – and especially your time*

The chapter concludes with a full-length Case Study which gives an idea of what to expect from the AAT pre-release material for the synoptic assessment.

INTRODUCTION TO THE UNIT

what this Unit involves

The Unit 'Accounting Systems and Controls' combines four AAT Learning Outcomes which will be assessed in a synoptic assessment:

- demonstrate understanding of the role and responsibilities of the accounting function within an organisation
- evaluate the internal control systems
- evaluate an organisation's accounting system and underpinning procedures
- analyse recommendations made to improve an organisation's accounting system

what you will learn

When you have completed this Unit you should be able to:

- **understand the role of accounting** in an organisation in supporting different departments of the organisation and dealing with outside organisations and individuals
- understand the importance and principles of **internal control** of the accounting function in an organisation – to help efficiency and to identify potential fraud and breaches of professional ethics
- **evaluate an accounting system** as part of a synoptic assessment
  - identifying the requirements of the accounting system
  - working out the improvements that could be made
  - making suggestions as to how the improvements could be implemented
  - identifying the impact that the changes would make on the system and its users
- **review a planned system change** and make suitable recommendations to ensure that the integrity of the system is maintained

what is a synoptic assessment?

The assessment takes the form of a **computer based synoptic assessment** submitted electronically to AAT for marking by the AAT.

The synoptic assessment consolidates and applies the knowledge and understanding gained from the mandatory Professional Diploma units of:

- Financial Statements of Limited Companies
- Management Accounting: Budgeting
- Management Accounting: Decision and Control

Students will be given pre-release material ahead of sitting the synoptic assessment to put the tasks within it into context. An example of such information is included at the end of this chapter.

The pre-release material will be based on a single business.

This synoptic assessment differs from the other assessments you will have encountered so far. It is not difficult, but it is challenging and it is different. It is recommended that you have studied Financial Statements of Limited Companies, Management Accounting: Budgeting, and Management Accounting: Decision and Control prior to tackling the synoptic assessment. This Accounting Systems and Controls Unit can be studied alongside these three units if required.

You will find this Unit will give you the opportunity to take on a new role – almost that of a consultant – and you can be creative in your approach and thinking. For this Unit, the synoptic assessment will include tasks where you:

- **review a current accounting system**, focusing on record keeping systems, principles of internal control, methods of fraud prevention and issues relating to professional ethics and sustainability
- **analyse a current accounting system**, identifying weaknesses or areas where improvement could be made and making recommendations to improve the system, bearing in mind all the costs involved

WHAT YOU WILL NEED TO KNOW – AN OVERVIEW

This section is intended to give you an idea of what you need to know for this part of the synoptic assessment. The chapters that follow broadly cover the material in this order. You should note that not every area will be covered in an individual synoptic assessment. However, over time, all areas will be tested so you need to ensure you are confident in every area prior to taking the synoptic assessment.

initial review of an organisation

To start with, you should:

- define the structure, purpose and organisation of the **accounting function** within the overall organisation
- identify the **relationship** between the accounting function and the other internal departments
- identify the important **external relationships** the organisation maintains; this could include relationships with customers, suppliers, shareholders, banks, trade organisations and governmental bodies such as HM Revenue & Customs
- decide **what an organisation requires from its accounting systems** – these requirements will differ depending on the nature and size of the organisation and will often be based on computer software solutions

review of the accounting system

You will need to **review part of the accounting system** to ensure that it meets the requirements of the organisation. In short . . .

- how good is it?
- do things go wrong?
- could things go wrong?

This review could involve:

- evaluating an accounting system including, for example, sales, purchases, credit control, payments and receipts, payroll, petty cash, capital expenditure, budgeting and management reporting
- identifying the **strengths and weaknesses** of part of the accounting system – this could include a review of the working methods used within the accounting system to ensure that the best results are being achieved especially in terms of cost-effectiveness, reliability and speed
- identifying the **external regulations** that will influence the way the accounting system will operate (eg legislation affecting payroll, or VAT regulations) and how the accounting function needs to adapt when they change
- **reviewing and evaluating the internal control system** by identifying areas where there is a potential for **error**

- **reviewing and evaluating the internal control system** by identifying areas where there is a potential for **fraud** involving loss of money, inventory or working time, and then assessing the level of risk of that fraud – ie how likely it is
- identifying **ways of detecting fraud** and the types of **internal controls** that could be established to **prevent fraud** occurring
- identifying breaches or threats to the fundamental principles of **professional ethics**, eg petty theft in the workplace
- assessing the extent to which the accounting system fulfils the requirements of **sustainability** principles (eg by recycling resources, saving energy and by encouraging cycling to work)
- **reviewing the weaknesses** that have been identified in the accounting system and explaining their impact upon the organisation – in terms of time, money and reputation (for example the loss of revenue, time wasting, letting customers down)
- reviewing where there is a **change in accounting system** to determine the controls needed to move from the old to new system

making recommendations

You may need to be able to make clear and sensible recommendations to rectify the weaknesses identified in your evaluation of the accounting systems:

- where you identify a weakness you need to offer a **recommendation** to rectify it
- you may be asked to work out the **comparative cost** of the recommendations you are making, for example the cost of training, new computers, and the benefits they will provide; the need for staff training is very important
- you may be asked to **present** and justify the changes you want to make to management

HOW TO TACKLE THE SYNOPTIC ASSESSMENT

The processes described so far – and the thought of sitting a synoptic assessment – may seem scary, but when you have finished this chapter you should be much more familiar with what is required and see how it all fits together.

There are three processes involved:

1 Be competent at the exams for the required Units

2 Learn the theory

3 Apply the theory

1 be competent at the exams for the required Units

As the synoptic assessment is testing several units of knowledge, as well as Accounting Systems and Controls, you need a sound knowledge of the three core subjects at Level 4 to help you pass it. The three subjects for which there are individual Osborne Books Tutorials and Workbooks are:

- Financial Statements of Limited Companies
- Management Accounting: Budgeting
- Management Accounting: Decision and Control

You should be **competent** in these areas prior to studying this Unit.

2 learning the theory

In order to be able to assess an organisation and its accounting system you will need to acquire basic knowledge about areas such as:

- types of organisation – their needs and links with the commercial world
- accounting systems – their areas of activity and how they link with the rest of the organisation
- internal control systems
- the dangers of fraud and the levels of risk involved
- effective accounting systems and how they produce reliable, accurate information
- the ethical code, set out by the AAT
- the need for sustainability and practical ways of achieving it
- cost-benefit analysis – how to assess the benefits of a recommendation in relation to its costs

All these theoretical areas are covered in the chapters that immediately follow this one. These are:

Chapter 2 **The accounting function – how it works**

This explains the way in which accounting systems work and how they support the organisation and how they relate to outside bodies.

Chapter 3 **Stakeholders and their information needs**

This explains the various stakeholders in an organisation and how the management information systems are designed to provide them all with the information they need.

Chapter 4 **Internal control systems and fraud**

This explains the way in which an organisation and its accounting system could exercise control over its operations and how to use ratios and performance indicators to help.

Chapter 5 **Preventing and detecting fraud**

This also explains the types of fraud and how it can affect organisations, as well as how to prevent and detect it.

Chapter 6 **Effective accounting systems**

This explains the different types of systems needed in an organisation and how they promote ethical and sustainable practices.

3 apply the theory – review the system and make recommendations

When you are confident of your knowledge in these areas, you will be able to:

- **review** an accounting system
- make **recommendations** for improvement
- assess the **benefits** of a recommendation in relation to its **costs**

This is covered in:

Chapter 7 **Evaluation and review of an accounting system**

This will explain how you can review and evaluate an accounting system and determine weaknesses within it.

Chapter 8 **Recommending and making changes**

This will explain the reasons for making changes to procedures and systems and the benefits of making them, along with any possible problems that may need resolving when changes are made.

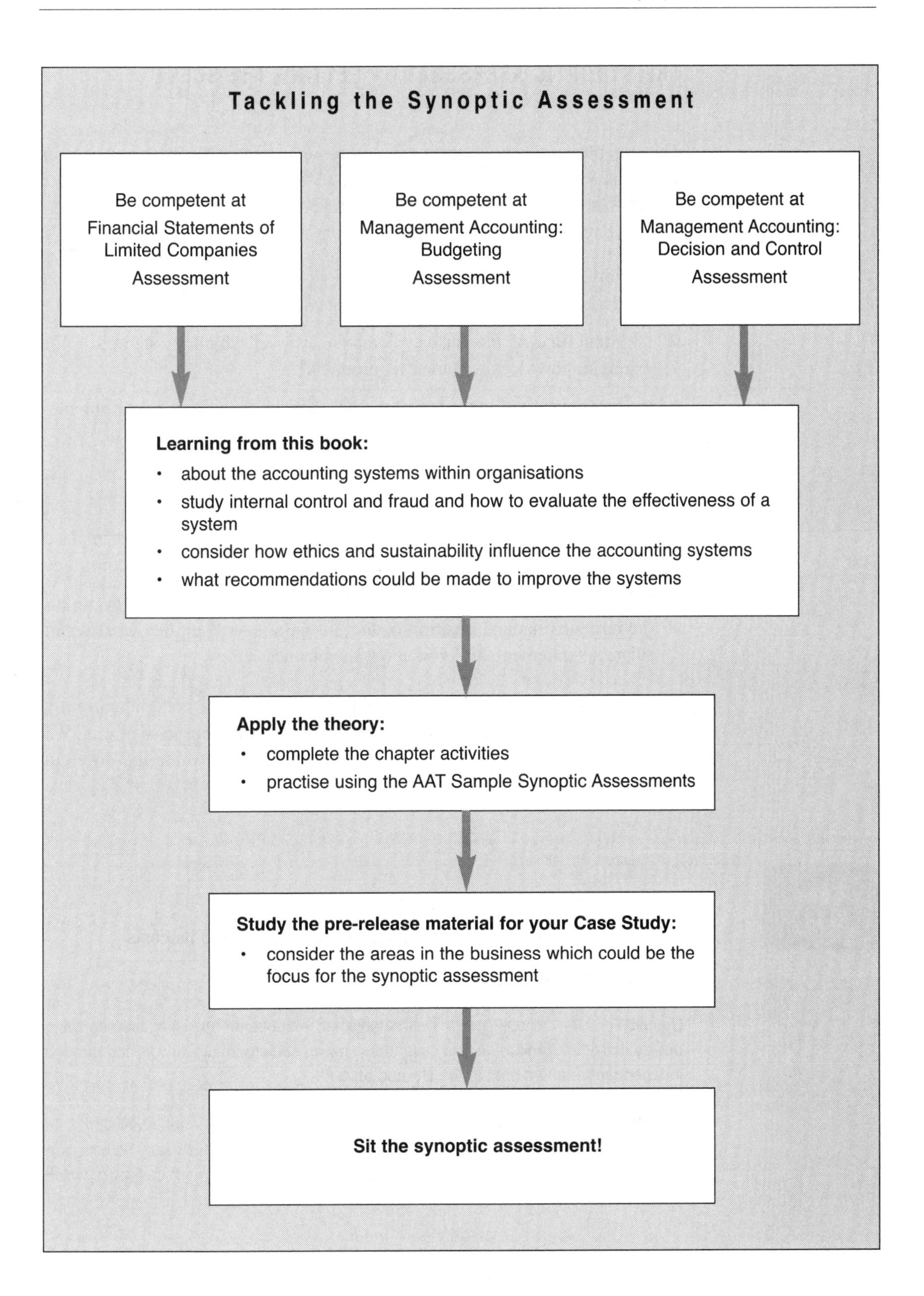
Tackling the Synoptic Assessment
Be competent at
Financial Statements of Limited Companies
Assessment
Be competent at
Management Accounting: Budgeting
Assessment
Be competent at
Management Accounting: Decision and Control
Assessment
Learning from this book:
• about the accounting systems within organisations
• study internal control and fraud and how to evaluate the effectiveness of a system
• consider how ethics and sustainability influence the accounting systems
• what recommendations could be made to improve the systems
Apply the theory:
• complete the chapter activities
• practise using the AAT Sample Synoptic Assessments
Study the pre-release material for your Case Study:
• consider the areas in the business which could be the focus for the synoptic assessment
Sit the synoptic assessment!

THE SYNOPTIC ASSESSMENT – SETTING THE SCENE

The synoptic assessment questions will be set around a business and to help you think about the issues it might face; the AAT has decided to give students access to some material prior to the day you sit the exam at the computer. This 'pre-release' material explains:

- the **industry** the business is involved in and how long the business has been trading for – is it new or established?
- the **structure** of the business and the way in which it operates – for example, how does it market its products?
- the **key personnel** in the business, including in the accounts department – are staff experienced or not? What size is it?
- recent **developments** in the market the company operates – is it fast moving, competitive or increasingly regulated?
- how the company monitors its **performance** – what measures are in place to monitor customer satisfaction, internal efficiency, employee performance and financial performance?
- the current financial position of the business – what do the latest set of financial statements tell you about the business?

The following Case Study follows the pattern of the AAT material currently available, to give you an idea of what you can analyse prior to the exam. We will use this business as we go through the book to illustrate the different aspects of the unit.

Case Study

DESIGN FOR LIFE LTD

Company background and history

Design For Life Ltd (DFL) is a well established manufacturing business, supplying quality designed furniture to end customers via two showrooms in the UK and through independent retailers both in the UK and abroad.

The company operates through a manufacturing division and a sales division. The manufacturing division supplies furniture to the sales division, which sells both its own manufactured product and other ranges of furniture that complement their own, which it buys in from third parties, some of which are imported.

DFL has its head office on an industrial estate in Exeter, where its management team and accounts department are both based. Its main manufacturing plant is also on this site, as are the sales division's offices and large central warehouse.

DFL was established forty years ago by two designers, Sigmund Rumney and Thomaz Whyte. Their children, Conrad Rumney and Edyta Whyte, then jointly owned and ran the business for several years before selling the shares two years ago. They no longer have a controlling interest but continue to work for the company.

Joseph Armstrong was brought into the company and joined the board as Finance Director just over one year ago to have more high-level professional accounting expertise, as the new owners were looking to expand the group.

Over the past forty years, the company has grown and in the year ended 31 December 20-1 it had a turnover of £10 million. It also now employs around 150 full-time equivalent employees, many of whom are skilled craftsmen. However, profits from operations have fallen in recent years.

In an attempt to improve profitability, DFL has recently acquired a controlling interest in Arc Ltd, a small manufacturing business that manufactures copyrighted designs of designer furniture that are complementary to those manufactured by DFL. Arc Ltd has prepared initial accounts for its first year of trading under the control of DFL. A management bonus is linked to these results but it has not yet been authorised for payment by DFL's remuneration committee.

DFL's mission statement

- We aim to be a market-focused business that specialises in the sourcing, production and distribution of well designed, quality furniture.
- Our priority is providing great service and a quality product range, designed to enhance the environment of people who own it.
- We aim to develop long-term relationships with all our stakeholders and deal with suppliers, customers and our staff with the highest levels of integrity.

Developments in the furniture market

During the past few years, the company has been feeling the effects of a recession. House sales have been poor, and customers have been unwilling to 'invest' in designer furniture. Intense competition from overseas manufacturers, made worse by the strength of the pound, has led to a downwards pressure on market prices within the areas in which DFL operates.

Over several years, several of DFL's key designs were copyrighted and have provided the core of the product range. These copyrights are due to expire soon and DFL need to invest in new designs, to hold their position in the market and, hopefully, improve it. This was a key reason for purchasing Arc Ltd.

DFL's strategic planning and control

When Joseph Armstrong joined DFL, he suggested that they need to view the business from different perspectives rather than just focus on its financial results. The directors and the controlling shareholders agreed to develop measures, collect data and judge the company's performance relative to each of these perspectives. These measures have now been in place for a full year and have just been reviewed.

Perspective 1

The first perspective involves employee training and having corporate cultural attitudes that reflect the time and skill require to design and create the product. An organisation, such as DFL relies on a highly skilled workforce, so its people are an important resource, as in a market requiring high quality and 'stand out' design, DFL need to ensure they have the right skills at design and production level to deliver the products required for today's customers.

Measures were put into place to focus training funds where they could help the most. This perspective recognises that 'craftsmanship' is more than 'training'; it also considers aspects like the effectiveness of mentoring within the organisation and 'up skilling' where possible to ensure continued availability of skilled labour and a strong design team.

In general, the first year's results show that the company has performed poorly in relation to this perspective.

Perspective 2

The second perspective refers to internal business processes. Measures based on this perspective allow the directors to see how well their business is running, and whether its products and services conform to customer requirements (as per its mission statement). The various line managers within DFL carefully designed these measures.

In general, the first year's results show that the company has performed well in relation to this perspective.

Perspective 3

The third perspective relates to how DFL's customers view the business. Edyta Whyte has stressed the importance of customer focus and customer satisfaction. She has emphasised that these are leading indicators; if customers are not satisfied, they will source other furniture that will meet their needs better. Poor performance on this perspective is therefore a key indicator of future decline, even though the current financial results may still look reasonable.

The first year's results indicate that customers were generally satisfied with the customer care and service, but were less satisfied with some of the older products in the product range, in terms of comfort and being suitable for the way customers use the furniture today.

Interestingly, customers were generally more satisfied with the bought-in products being sold by the sales division than those manufactured in-house by DFL itself. There was considerable interest in the new products manufactured by Arc Ltd.

Perspective 4

The fourth and final perspective is the traditional outlook using financial data. Joseph Armstrong instigated the use of more accurate and timely monthly management accounts immediately after he was appointed. He argued that the previous focus on only financial data had led to an "unbalanced" situation with no attention having been paid to the real drivers of business performance.

The financial results continue to show falling profits which the other perspectives help to explain.

Strategy-mapping

DFL has used the first year's results to carry out a strategy-mapping exercise (strategy maps are communication tools used to tell a story of how value is created for the organisation. They show a logical, step-by-step connection between strategic objectives in the form of causes and effects).

Generally speaking, improving performance in the objectives from the first of DPL's perspectives will enable it to improve its results for customer satisfaction and eventually its financial performance.

This implies that DFL needs to reallocate resources towards increasing its training and design spend; which will, in turn, redirect its internal processes towards new designs and product development. This should result in improved customer satisfaction and retention, with the final outcome being increased profitability.

Some of the directors, however, believe that the root cause of DFL's problems are due to the Finance Director – ie the problems are due to poor internal controls and systemic weaknesses. The directors also point out that they will struggle to finance any significant increase in improving the design and production processes.

At this point in time, the board is divided and uncertain how to move the business forward.

Staff

SLP's key personnel are as follows:

Managing Director	Conrad Black
Finance Director	Joseph Armstrong
Production Director	David Duke
Sales Director	Edyta White
Chief Accountant	Aneysha Dickson
Purchasing Manager	Matt Arnold
Warehouse Manager	Andrew Roberts
Credit Controller	Salam Khan
Accounts Payable Clerk	Tina Fay
Accounts Receivable Clerk	Lila Firkin
General Accounts Clerk and Cashier	Ricardo Cox
Payroll Clerk	Petra Stanya

SLP's financial statements

The financial statements for SLP for the year ended 31 December 20-1 show that the company had a turnover of £10 million, and made a profit after tax of £963,000. These accounts do not include the results of Arc Ltd, which was acquired on 1 January 20-2.

Group statement of profit or loss for the year ended 31 December 20-1

Continuing Operations	*£000*
Revenue	10,000
Cost of Sales	(6,600)
Gross Profit	3,400
Operating expenses	(2,150)
Profit from operations	1,250
Finance costs	(75)
Profit before tax	1,175
Tax	(212)
Profit for the period from continuing operations	963

Group Statement of Financial Position at 31 December 20-1

	£000
ASSETS	
Non-current assets	
Property, plant and equipment	3,120
	3,120
Current assets	
Inventories	1,514
Trade receivables	1,841
Cash and cash equivalents	150
	3,505
Total assets	6,625
EQUITY AND LIABILITIES	
Equity	
Ordinary share capital (£1 shares)	50
Share premium	780
Retained earnings	3,652
Total equity	4,482
Non-current liabilities	
Bank loans	630
	630
Current liabilities	
Trade payables	1,356
Tax liabilities	157
	1,513
Total liabilities	2,143
Total equity and liabilities	6,625

2 The accounting function – how it works

this chapter covers...

In this chapter we examine the way in which the accounting function 'fits into' the overall structure of the organisation and how it relates to other organisations.

The areas the chapter covers include:

- *how what an organisation does – ie its 'business' – affects its accounting function*
- *the overall structure of the organisation*
- *the structure of the accounting system*
- *how the accounting system interacts with the other functions*
- *the administrative systems and control of resources within the organisation*
- *the uses of the financial statements of the organisation*
- *the effect on an accounting system of changes brought about by external regulations*

THE 'BUSINESS' OF THE ORGANISATION

public and private sectors

Organisations are normally classed as public sector or private sector.

Public sector organisations are those owned or controlled directly or indirectly by the state. They include corporations like the BBC, Government Departments and local authorities. Their function is largely to provide some form of service: broadcasting, health, education, policing, refuse collection, tax collection, for example. Some public sector organisations form partnerships with private sector companies to provide a service, eg hospitals in the National Health Service.

Private sector organisations, on the other hand, are in private ownership, and include businesses ranging from the sole trader to the public limited company. The function of these organisations is to provide a product such as a car or TV or a service such as a holiday or a foot massage.

The range of activities carried out by both public and private sector organisations – the nature of their 'business' can therefore be classified as:

- providing goods – either through manufacturing or through retailing
- providing a service – either for consumers (private sector) or as a social benefit (public sector)

You may not consider that tax collection is a social benefit, but if you appreciate that tax revenue is used for Government spending on health and education, you will see the logic.

how the 'business' affects the accounting system

All organisations need accounting systems to carry out the accounting function. This function includes:

- processing and recording financial transactions – keeping accounts
- payroll
- costing and budgeting
- raising finance

You will see from this list that these are 'generic' functions which are common to all organisations. The variation is in the detail and will depend on the type of 'business' the organisation carries out:

- a manufacturing company in the private sector, for example, will keep accounts for suppliers and customers, will run payroll and will cost and budget for the manufacturing process and other activities; it is likely to raise finance from banks and possibly the equity markets

- a local authority in the public sector will keep accounts for suppliers and to a lesser extent for customers (council tax payers), it will run payroll and keep to strict budgets; its financing, however, will come from Central Government, local enterprises and from local taxation

We will look at effective accounting systems in Chapter 5 and consider how to evaluate an accounting system in Chapter 6.

ORGANISATIONAL STRUCTURE

The organisation of the accounting system will depend a great deal on the way in which the organisation as a whole is structured.

In the case of a smaller organisation such as a private company the structure will be based on the shareholder directors being in charge of the whole business, with possibly a finance director in charge of the finance and accounting function. The variation arises when the organisation is larger, in which case the structure is likely to be either:

- a loosely organised group of independent operating units, directed by a managing company, or
- driven from the top and tightly controlled as a single unit

These are represented by the two basic types of organisational structure: flat and hierarchical.

flat structure – large organisation

This is where operating divisions of an organisation are relatively independent, and are likely to have their own accounting systems. A typical example is where groups of companies are divided up in terms of geographical areas or products. It must be stressed that it will be the responsibility of the managing company to ensure that the accounting systems of the separate companies are harmonised and work together. Study the diagram below.

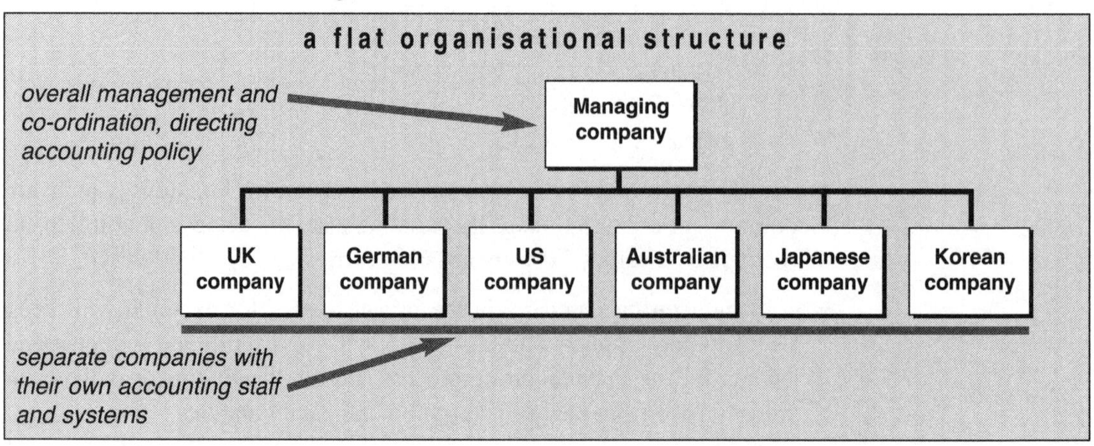

hierarchical structure – large organisation

A hierarchy is a series of levels of people, each level controlled by the level above it. This structure – also known as a 'tall' structure – is suitable for a large organisation such as a public limited company or Government Department which may have thousands of employees. In this type of structure the accounting system will be the responsibility of the Finance Director and is centralised and strictly controlled. Study the diagram below.

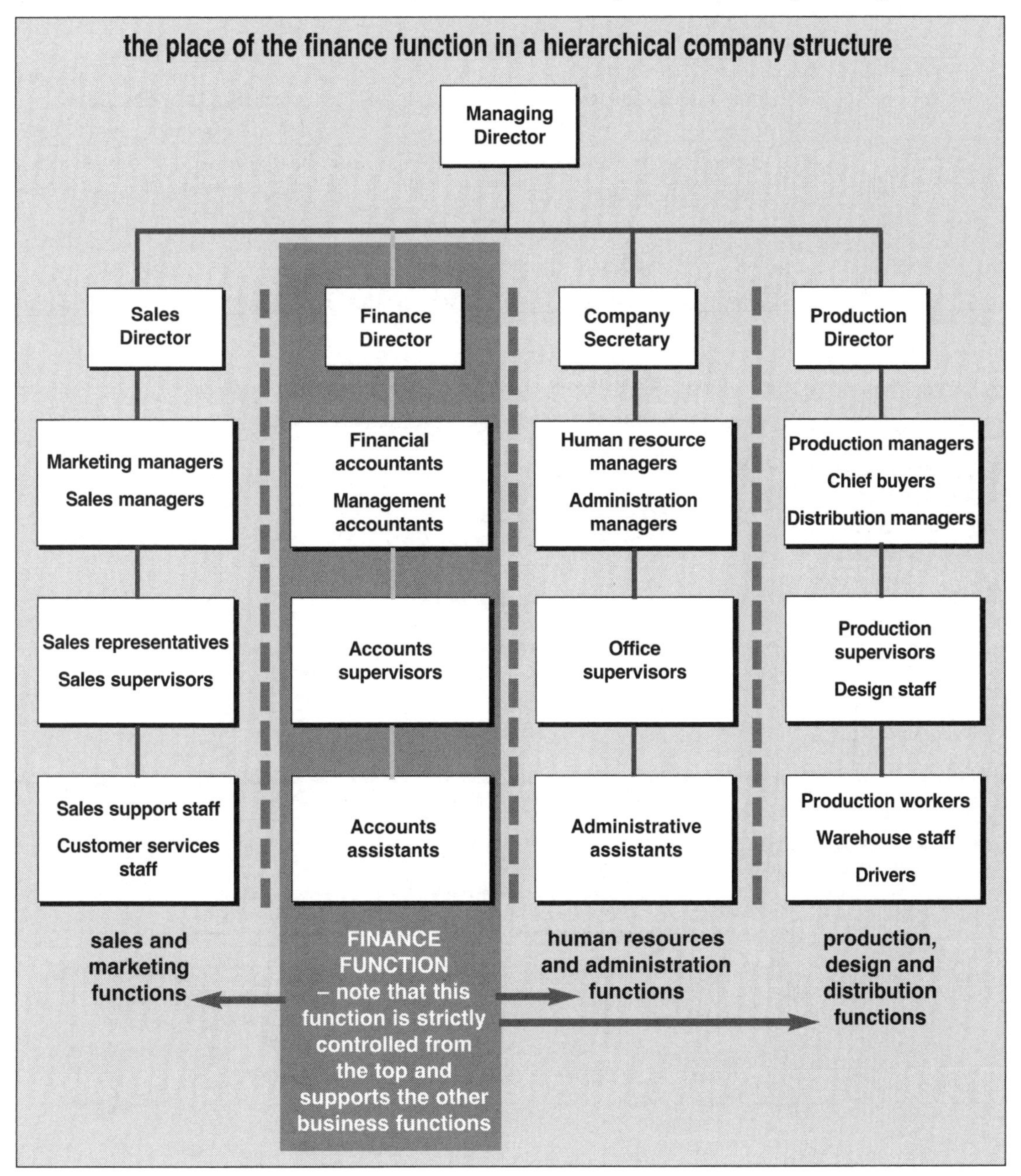

organisational structure – small business

It is appreciated that this chapter has so far concentrated on large organisations. It is possible that the business provided in the AAT synoptic assessment will be a **smaller business** or **voluntary organisation**. The large majority of businesses in the UK are, in fact, small businesses with fifty or fewer employees.

The organisational structure of a small business is more likely to be 'flat' with the boss at the top and a variety of 'functions' or small departments under his or her direct control.

One of these functions will, of course, be the **accounting function**. This may involve a line manager who oversees a number of assistants and reports directly to the business owner. It may also be the case that the business owner looks after some of the accounting functions himself/herself, for example negotiating discounts and credit terms with major customers or completing the VAT Return.

This type of business is illustrated in the 'flat structure business' diagram below.

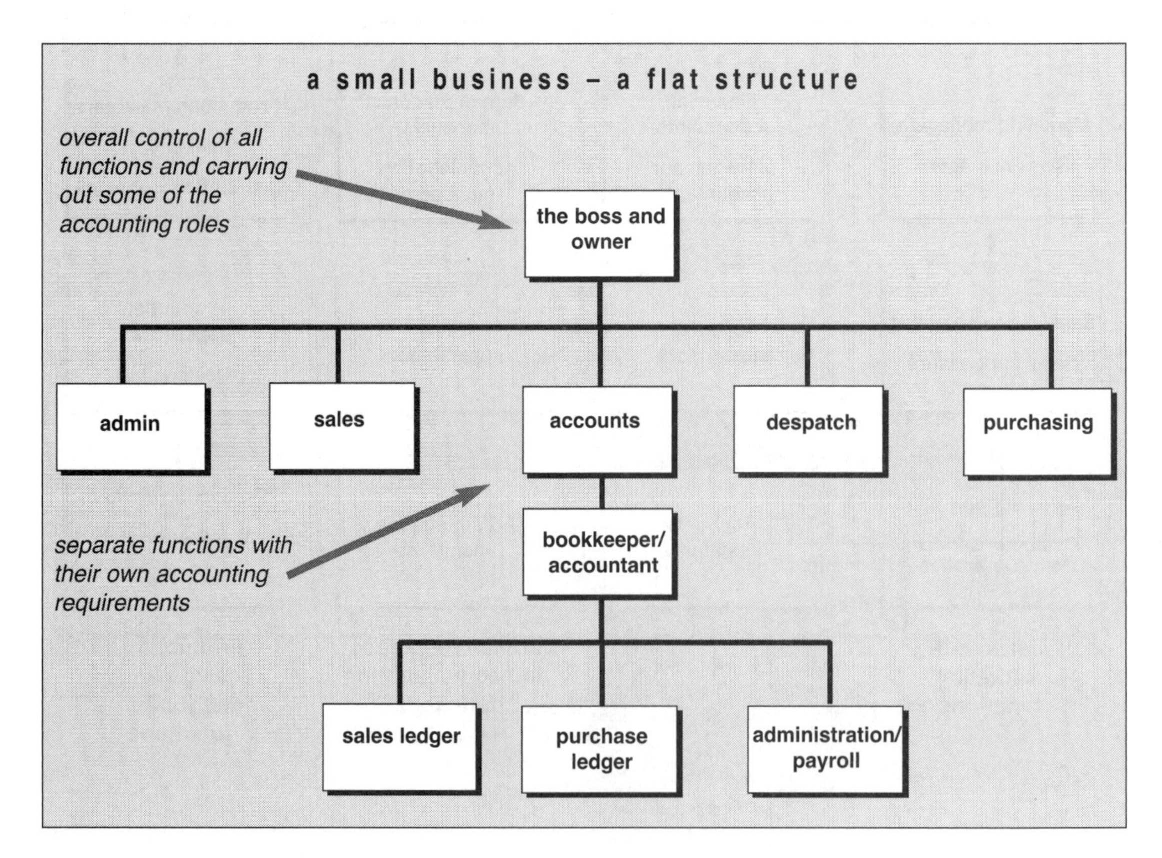

Case Study

DESIGN FOR LIFE LTD: ORGANISATIONAL STRUCTURE

situation

Have a look back at the material for our example business on pages 10 to 15. Draw the organisational structure for this business.

solution

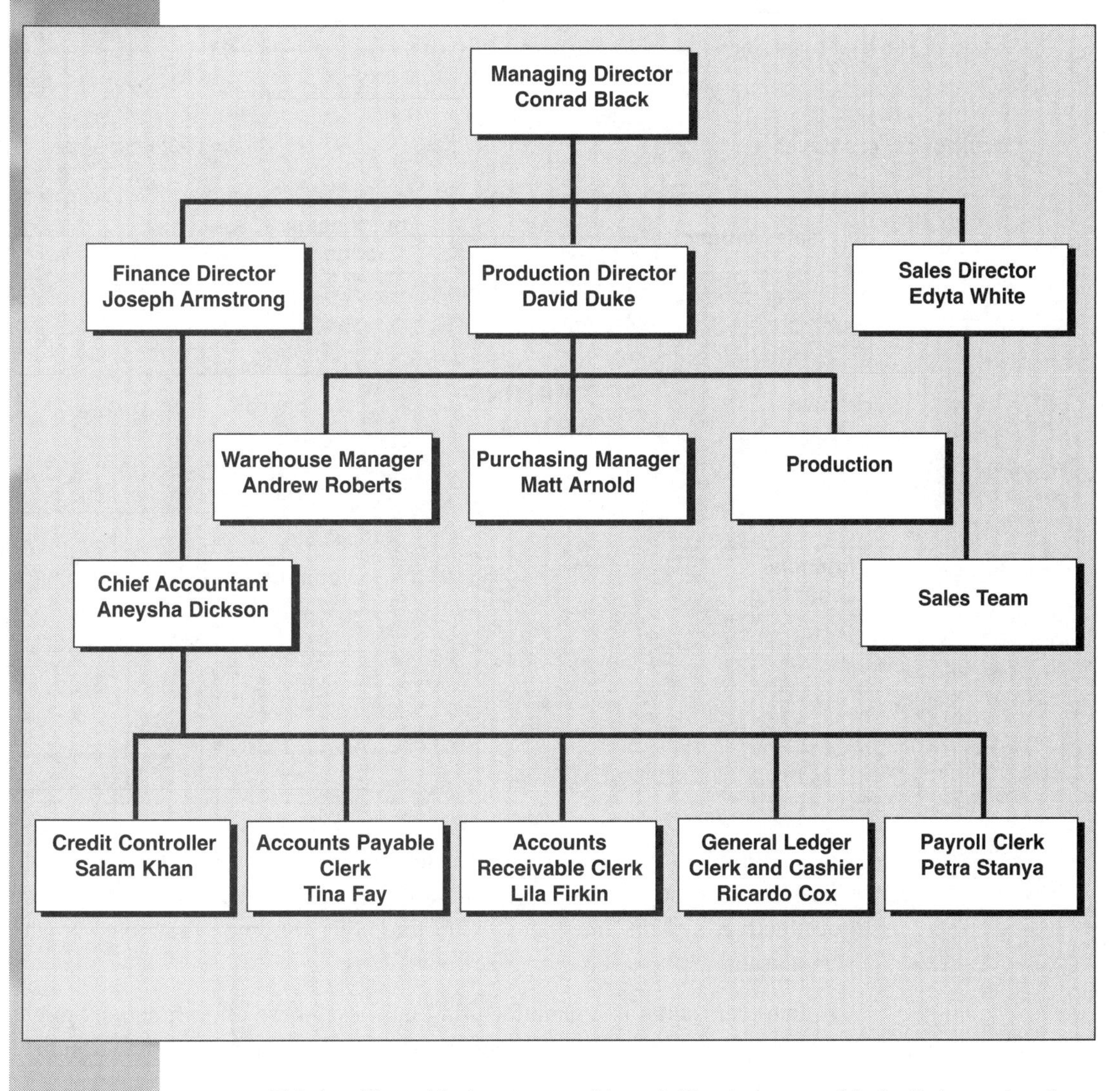

This is a hierarchical structure, with each Director responsible for their own function.

FUNCTIONS OF AN ACCOUNTING SYSTEM

The synoptic assessment requires you to look critically at the existing accounting system and to identify areas for improvement in both the system itself and the way in which it is managed.

A typical accounting system carries out a number of functions, shown in the diagram below. It is the responsibility of the management to ensure that it operates smoothly.

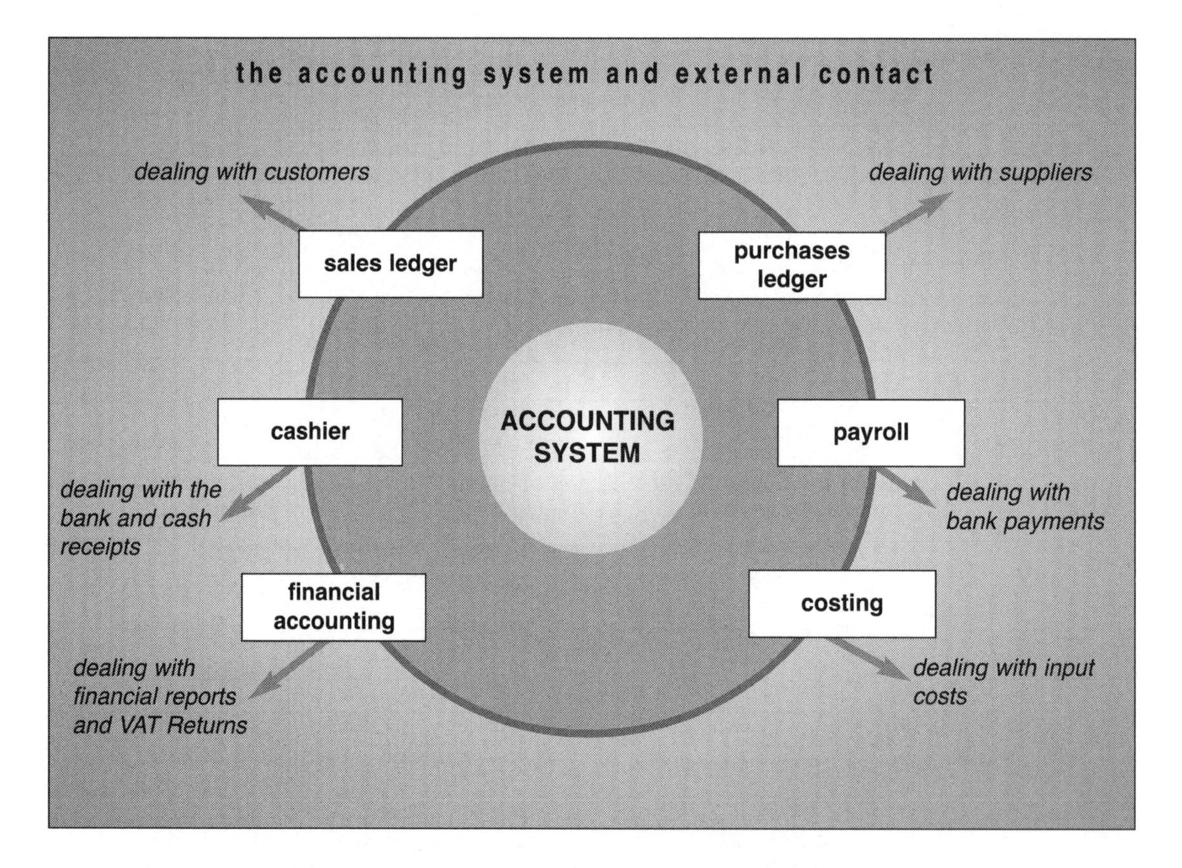

It is important that the accounting system is not seen to operate in isolation. Part of the synoptic assessment may be to analyse the way in which the accounting system integrates with the other internal functions of the organisation.

If the organisation is a manufacturing business, these other functions might include production, human resources, sales and marketing, administration.

Study the diagram on the next page to see how the accounting system interrelates with some of the other internal functions of the organisation.

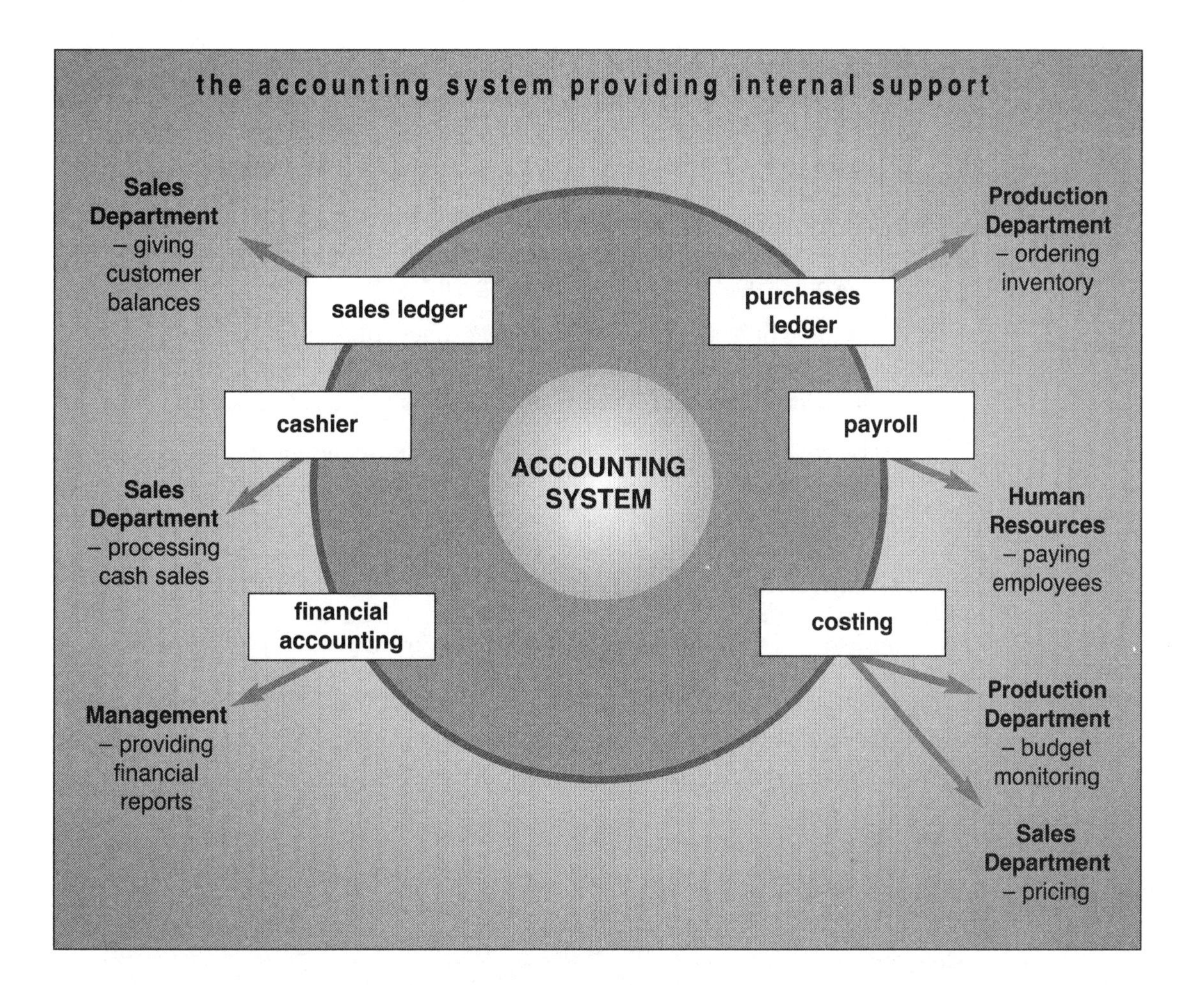

Answering the synoptic assessment

When you evaluate the accounting system of the organisation you will need to analyse the way in which the organisation structures its accounting system. Some form of structure chart would be a useful aid, and could be produced using the pre-release material given to you by the AAT.

Your analysis might consider weaknesses in the way the system is structured, in the way it is managed and in the way in which it communicates with people – eg customers or suppliers – **outside** the organisation.

Your analysis should also look at the way in which the accounting system deals with other functions **inside** the organisation. A good starting point is to look at communications between the various departments. Is the system at fault at all?

THE NEED FOR GOOD COMMUNICATION

lines of communication in an accounting system

You will need to analyse the effectiveness of the communication between people in the accounting function itself – in addition to the communication between people in other functions, eg sales.

The diagram below illustrates the lines of communication between accounting employees in a large company. The accounting system here is subdivided into the areas of financial and management accounting.

The boxes with the dark grey background all represent specific accounting roles. You will see that the structure is set out in a series of layers of authority and responsibility.

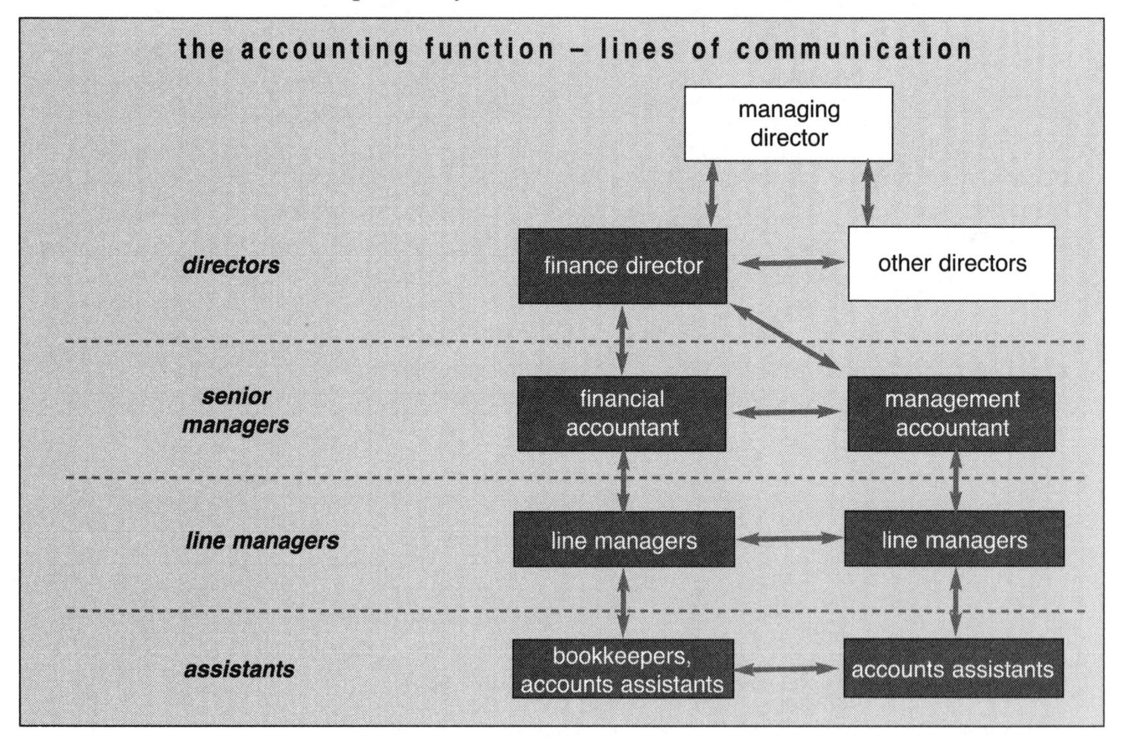

CONTROL OF RESOURCES BY INDIVIDUALS IN THE ORGANISATION

the need for resources

Adequate **resources** are essential to the functioning of an organisation. All come at a cost. Resources can be classified under four main headings:

- **equipment and material resources**

  These include premises in which to work and equipment needed on a day-to-day basis. They also include the materials that may be used – raw materials, inventory and consumables such as biros and photocopy paper. A car manufacturer will clearly have a greater need for equipment and material resources in a factory than a firm of insurance brokers working from a town centre office. The important point here is that in both cases the resources will need to be adequate.

- **human resources**

  This term is now used widely to describe the 'people' function in organisations. There is always a need for the right number of appropriately skilled people to work within an organisation, whether in a management or an operational role.

- **information**

  This is an essential resource and must be readily available to whoever needs it within the organisation. Computer-based systems with up-to-date and accurate information are the ideal solution (see last section). Information in a manufacturing or retail business, for example, will include product specifications, prices, inventory levels, customer orders, supplier orders. A travel agency will need different types of information, but equally, the data will need to be accurate and up-to-date and on computer screen.

- **financial resources**

  This term means 'money' which is either available currently or can be made available within a set time period to allow spending in line with a particular budget allocation. This is probably the most critical type of resource for the functioning of the organisation. It affects all areas.

control of resources by individuals

As part of your synoptic assessment you may examine the way in which individuals within the organisation control the supply of the various resources described above. Control of resources is normally dictated by the various levels of budget within an organisation.

For example, the production or staffing budget of a business is likely to be decided upon at director level and the departmental budget will be the responsibility of the departmental manager. Line managers (supervisors) will also have decisions to make about control of resources – for example they may be given the power to allow staff to work overtime and to order small items of office equipment. Employees at assistant level will also have control of resources at a reduced level, for example ordering stationery items or tea and coffee for the rest room. It is all a question of level and scale.

The diagram below sets out the hierarchy of individuals who will make decisions about controlling resources; it shows 'level and scale'.

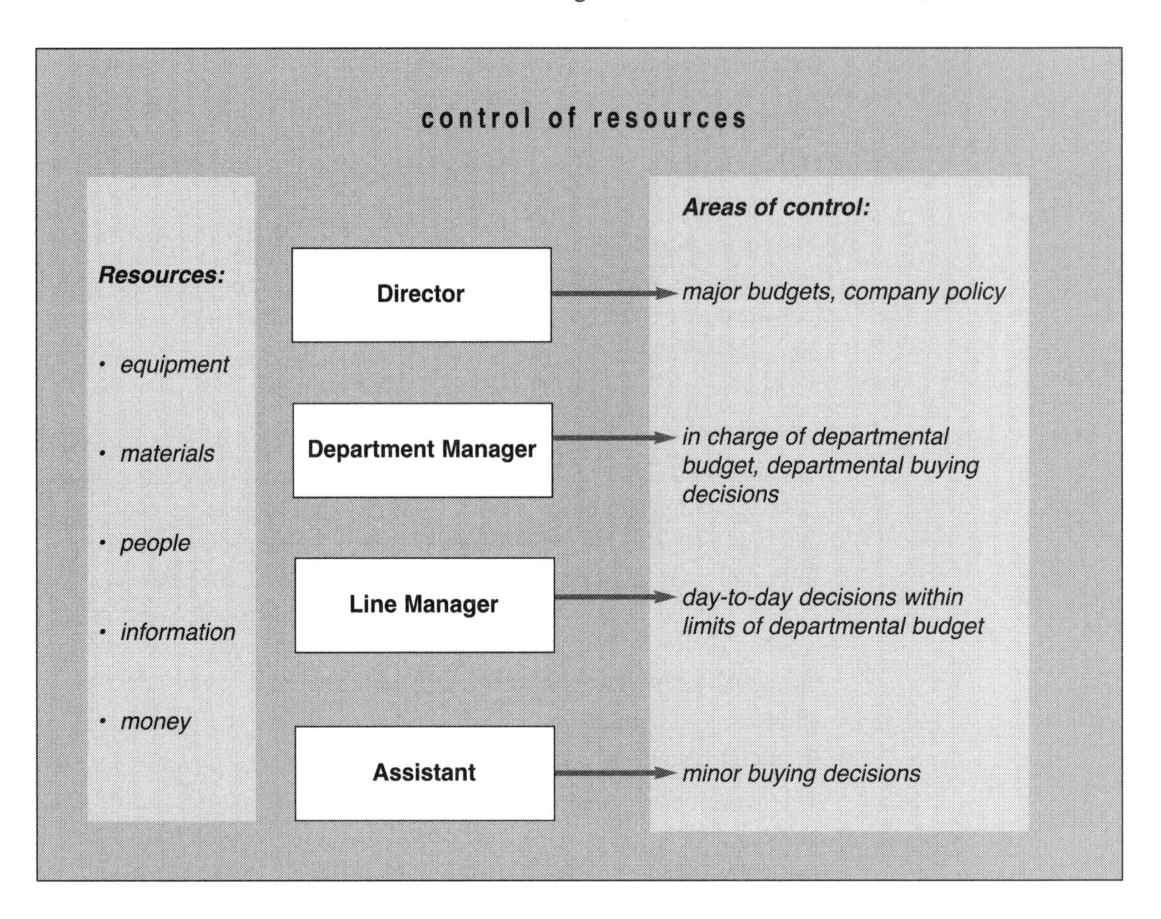

errors and fraud within the system

The control of resources brings with it the opportunity both for error and for fraud. Both can be avoided with the enforcement of checking and monitoring procedures. **Error** includes situations involving over-ordering of materials – for example ordering 5,000 suspension files instead of 100 where the units ordered were boxes of 50 rather than individual files. **Fraud** is a fact of life where control of resources is concerned. It can range from a director siphoning off funds by 'fiddling the books' to the supposedly innocent pilfering of biros and stationery at assistant level. The issue of fraud is covered in detail in Chapter 5.

FINANCIAL ACCOUNTS AND MANAGEMENT ACCOUNTS

As part of the synoptic assessment, you will need to consider whether the business is able to produce the accounting information it needs in a timely and accurate manner. This information could be either in the form of financial accounts or management account information. The key elements of each of these are considered below.

financial accounts

Most organisations produce Financial Accounts at the end of each year, to enable external users to understand the performance and financial position of the business. In the case of a limited company, this is the legal or statutory responsibility of the Directors. During the year, the financial transactions of the business are recorded by the accounts team. At the year-end, these financial transactions in the business are presented in a set of accounts in the required format.

The key financial statements that are usually produced are:

- the statement of profit or loss (also known as the income statement)
- the statement of financial position
- the statement of cash flows

Financial statements are produced:

- for **internal use** by the organisation for planning and budgeting reasons
- for **external use** to provide information to stakeholders such as banks, shareholders, suppliers, customers, employees, possible investors and Government bodies such as HMRC.

The Level 4 Unit Financial Statements of Limited Companies shows how to produce company accounts and what they include in detail.

Answering the synoptic assessment

As part of the pre-release material for the synoptic assessment you will be given a set of financial statements and may need to analyse them. We will look at who might want the results of this analysis in the next chapter.

management accounts

Management accounts use the same transactional data to produce information for internal use to allow the director and managers to control and manage the business. This information is often produced on a daily, weekly or monthly basis, in any format the business requires, to help those who read it to understand the financial implications of decisions they are making. It can be looking at the recent past or considering future decisions.

For example, a budget may be produced at the start of the year to help managers plan resources, production schedules and prices. During the year managers may be monitored against this budget and variances calculated to see whether the business needs to adjust its plans due to changes in the market or economy. A forecast may be prepared based on performance to date to assist in the decision making process. Later on in Chapter 3 we will look at the types of report that managers and other internal stakeholders may need.

COMPLYING WITH EXTERNAL REGULATION

Complying with external regulations is very important to a business. If it does not comply, it could become liable to fines or legal action. The accounts department will be structured to ensure the staff who may be affected by such regulations are able to monitor them and make appropriate changes when needed.

For example the Financial Accountant will be responsible for monitoring compliance with Accounting Standards, which you will have studied already.

The Payroll Clerk will be trained in the latest tax rates, set out in the Finance Act, to ensure income tax is deducted correctly from individuals and paid on time to HMRC. The Accounts Receivable Clerk will know which sales attract VAT and at what rate.

Changes may be required because of the introduction of new external regulations or changes to existing rules.

Whatever the case, the accounting system should be ready to react to any external changes and have the internal policies and procedures established and in hand in order to be able to deal with them. Examples include:

- **changes in accounting terminology and accounting standards**

  You will know from your studies that there is move away from UK GAAP accounting terminology to international terminology which has been established by the International Accounting Standards Board (IASB) through its IASs and IFRSs. These are currently applicable to larger limited companies in the UK. It is likely that this terminology will eventually supersede the existing UK GAAP terminology, meaning that more and more organisations over time will need to refer to 'trade receivables' rather than 'debtors' and to 'inventory' rather than to 'stock.'

  Organisations will need to amend much documentation and invest in staff training to cope with these changes. Again, internal policies and procedures will need to be established to deal with this.

- **a change in company law**

  Company law in the UK was amended with the passing of the Companies Act 2006. This affected the way in which limited companies operated and included provisions which affected their accounting systems. For example, the requirement for authorised share capital was abolished – this affected the Statement of Financial Position.

  Companies and their advisors will therefore need to be alert to this type of change in legislation

- **a change in the VAT rate**

  This can seriously disturb the smooth running of any VAT-registered business. It particularly affects retail businesses, involving the repricing of goods on the shelf and in the warehouse, reprinting of catalogues, amendments on the website, amendments to invoicing software and the training of staff to deal with a confused public. The accounting function affected most would be accounts receivable, accounts payable and cash book.

  Most large retailers will have internal policies and procedures in hand to deal with this situation.

Chapter Summary

- The organisational structure will influence how the accounting system will be set up. Flat structures will have autonomous companies with separate accounts departments, which may include few staff – eg Sales Ledger, Purchase Ledger, Accountant. Hierarchical structures may have thousands of employees and several types of accounting employees eg Accounts Clerks, Accounts Assistants and Accounts Managers.

- The nature of the business determines which functions the accounting department carry out eg payroll, costing and budgeting, raising finance.

- Each function will support different areas of the business eg Sales ledger will give information to sales, Payroll will liaise with Human Resources.

- Good communication is vital for the accounts department to collect and deal with the information needed to produce accurate, timely financial information. Accounts will deal with all departments in the organisation to allow them to do this.

- Resources allow the business to meet its needs and objectives and can include equipment, people, information and finance.

- Financial statements are produced using the accounting systems by the directors, primarily for external users. You will be given some financial statements in the pre-release material, to help you understand the business.

- Financial statements usually include a statement of profit or loss, statement of financial position and statement of cash flows.

- Management accounts are only for internal use and may be in any format the business needs. They are produced using the same information used for the financial statements. Information may be produced daily, weekly or monthly.

- External regulations need to be complied with and the accounting function ensures this by including this responsibility within specific job roles. For example Payroll staff are knowledgeable in income tax rules, sales ledger staff in VAT rules.

- When external regulations, such as accounting standards, Companies Law and the Finance Act change, this may require the accounts department to make changes to their working practices to ensure the business continues to comply with them. The relevant staff will be responsible for ensuring they are made.

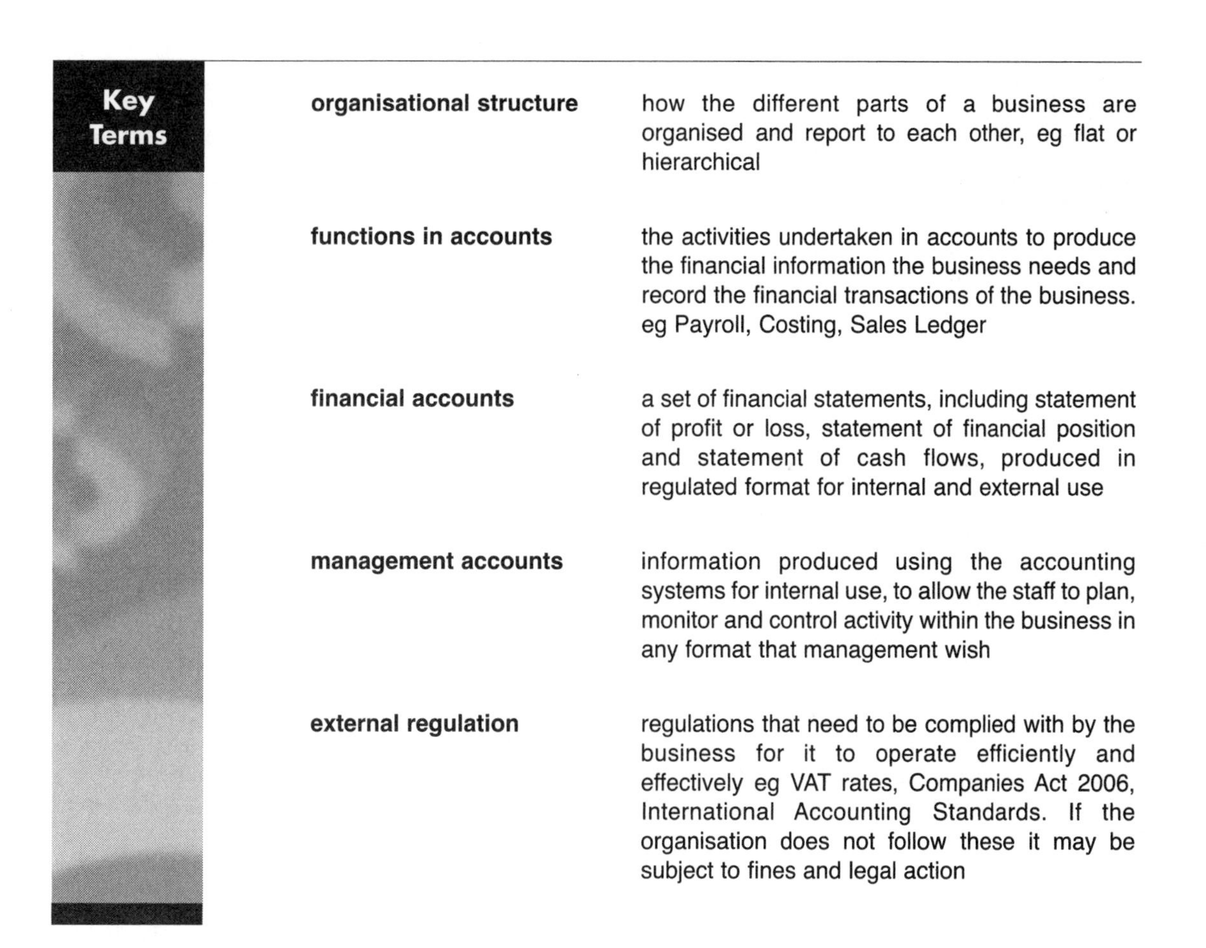

Key Terms

organisational structure — how the different parts of a business are organised and report to each other, eg flat or hierarchical

functions in accounts — the activities undertaken in accounts to produce the financial information the business needs and record the financial transactions of the business. eg Payroll, Costing, Sales Ledger

financial accounts — a set of financial statements, including statement of profit or loss, statement of financial position and statement of cash flows, produced in regulated format for internal and external use

management accounts — information produced using the accounting systems for internal use, to allow the staff to plan, monitor and control activity within the business in any format that management wish

external regulation — regulations that need to be complied with by the business for it to operate efficiently and effectively eg VAT rates, Companies Act 2006, International Accounting Standards. If the organisation does not follow these it may be subject to fines and legal action

Activities

2.1 Who has the statutory duty to prepare accounts for a limited company? Tick the appropriate options below.

(a) The company's auditors	
(b) The directors of the company	
(c) The Chief Accountant	
(d) Companies House	

2.2 Watkins Recruitment Limited is a firm specialising in providing recruitment services for its clients based in Berkshire and London. It is run by the two owners, William Watkins and Harry Watkins, who employ fifteen staff, including one who is responsible for accounts within the business. They are internet-based, hiring meeting rooms when needed on an ad-hoc basis to meet candidates or clients.

(a) List the main activities Watkins Recruitment Limited would have to account for and the main accounting functions.

(b) What type of structure would you expect Watkins Recruitment Limited to have and why?

2.3 Footy for Fun Limited is a manufacturer of table football games. They have two divisions, one of which manufactures a range of quality products from standalone tables to small games you can put onto an ordinary table and play. This division sells to high street retailers and internet distributors. The other division designs and makes custom football tables, which are sold all over the world and made to order. Both divisions are based in a factory in St Albans and the business employs 400 people.

(a) Identify the main activities Footy for Fun Limited would have to account for and the main accounting functions.

(b) What type of organisational structure would you expect Footy for Fun Limited to have and why?

2.4 Train Travel Limited runs a train operating company delivering travel in Surrey, Sussex, Kent and Hampshire. It has been operating for several years and employs several thousand people. The Finance Act has recently changed the rates wages are taxed at, the tax free allowances available and also employees are now taxed on the entire value of any travel discounts they might have as part of their employment as if they were a wage payment. Some discounts are of considerable value for Train Travel Limited's employees. The business has a dedicated Payroll Team, run by a Payroll Manager.

(a) What type of organisational structure do you think Train Travel Limited might have and why?

(b) Draft an email from the Payroll Manager to the Payroll Team, stating what changes might be needed to ensure the business continues to comply with payroll legislation.

2.5 If there was a change in VAT which was not implemented, who would be held responsible by HMRC?

(a)	The Finance Director	
(b)	The Sales Director	
(c)	The Managing Director	
(d)	All of the Directors	

3 Stakeholders and their information needs

this chapter covers...

In this chapter we examine the different stakeholders of the business, both external and internal and the type of information they may wish to use in order to keep up-to-date with the way in which the business is performing and being run.

The areas the chapter covers include:

- *the different types of stakeholders, both external and internal*
- *how the management information is designed to fit the needs of the business*
- *the types of information stakeholders might use including financial statements, management accounts and budgetary reporting*
- *the calculation of key performance indicators, including ratios*
- *the importance of ethics and sustainability when producing information for stakeholders*

The synoptic assessment could test this area in a variety of ways and it is important you are confident in suggesting, calculating and explaining suitable key performance indicators and ratios in particular.

STAKEHOLDERS – EXTERNAL AND INTERNAL

A stakeholder is a person or organisation that has an 'interest' in another organisation.

Stakeholders can be **internal** (eg employees, managers) or **external** (eg shareholders, banks, customers, suppliers, the tax authorities). Let us look at external stakeholders initially.

Take for example a retail organisation such as an electrical supermarket chain which is also a public limited company quoted on the stockmarket.

The functioning of the accounting system will be affected by external stakeholders in a number of ways:

- **customers** will need to be provided with easy and efficient means of making payment, and in suitable circumstances, credit terms and finance
- **suppliers** will need to be paid on time and credit terms and discounts will need to be negotiated and administered
- **banks** that are lending money to the company are likely to require regular (eg monthly) management accounts, eg levels of sales, inventory, cash held, payables, receivables
- the **tax authorities** (HM Revenue & Customs – a Government Department) will require calculation and payment of Corporation Tax, Value Added Tax and collection of Income Tax and National Insurance through the PAYE system
- **shareholders** will require information about the financial performance of the company in the form of an annual financial report in paper format or downloadable from the company's website
- **trade associations** will request financial statistics such as sales trends, details of exports, wage rates and so on for their regular trade reports

The relationship of an organisation with its external stakeholders is shown in the diagram set out on the next page.

Stakeholders can also be internal to the business:

- employees will want to know how well the business is performing and therefore if their jobs are likely to be secure in the future. If they have bonus-related pay, they will want information to help them work out if they are likely to be paid the bonus at the end of each bonus period eg weekly, monthly or yearly
- managers will need to be given information to allow them to manage the business effectively. For example, sales figures by branch could help them decide which branches are performing well and which need to improve. If branch staff are paid partly by bonus, performance information would be very important to them as well

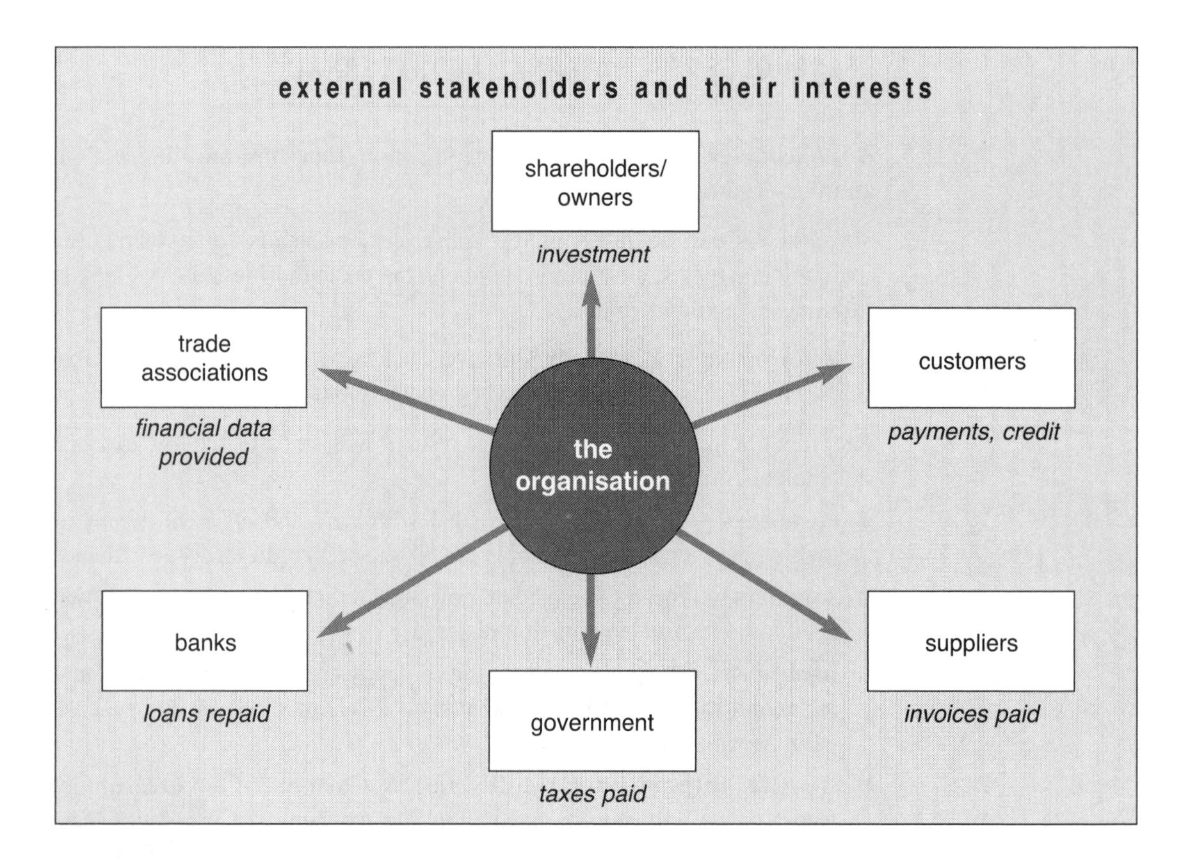

Case Study

COMFORTABLE KENNELS

situation

Florence and Rebecca Carter have run 'Comfortable Kennels' for several years. They cater for dogs, whose owners go on holiday for up to a month, marketing the kennels as 'a home from home'. They have looked after many of the same animals for several years and have a good working relationship with the local vet. Food and other essentials are supplied by a local pet store and delivered weekly.

They have recently invested in some new kennels (with large exercise areas attached), securing funding from the local branch of the Black Pony Bank. They have also taken on two new staff, now employing eight in total.

Identify the main internal and external stakeholders of Comfortable Kennels and explain why they are important.

solution

The main internal stakeholders are Florence and Rebecca and the eight staff they employ. They are all interested in how well the business is run and how profitable it is, as they want to have long-term security of their earnings.

There are several external stakeholders:

- The customers are interested, as they want the kennels to continue to provide a service for their dogs, some of which are old and may not like to go to a new kennels.
- The Vet will want the business to be successful so Comfortable Kennels will continue to be a customer and he can provide vet services to them in the future.
- The local pet store will also want the business to continue to trade so they can also continue to sell to them.
- HMRC will want to verify the business is paying the correct tax liabilities, regarding payroll, VAT and income tax
- Finally the bank will be concerned with the financial performance of the business as it will need to ensure that it will receive all the finance charges and repayments for the loan.

MANAGEMENT INFORMATION

management information systems (MIS)

A large organisation is often served by a **management information system (MIS).** This is a computer-based system which provides up-to-date, accurate and relevant information to management. An efficient MIS will enable management to make informed decisions promptly.

By 'management' we mean all levels of management, from line managers (supervisors) through to the Finance Director. Clearly the type and level of information required will vary according to the role of the manager and the type of decision expected of that manager. Examples of the type of data produced by an accounting MIS include:

- sales figures for products and regions
- inventory levels
- customer account details, ranging from balances to detailed reports such as the Aged Trade Receivables Analysis
- budgetary control reports showing variances
- profitability reports by product

You will see from this range of information that decision-making can range from 'Do we allow this customer any more credit?' through to 'Do we continue to manufacture this product?'

INTERNAL STAKEHOLDERS AND THEIR INFORMATION NEEDS

Management accounts and budgetary controls

Many organisations use management information systems to produce monthly management accounts, in any format that seems appropriate for their managers to use. An example of a layout of a set of management accounts is given below:

Modern Machinery Limited

Management Accounts for the month of October 20-1

	Flexed budget		**Actual**		**Variance**
Volume (units)	2,600,000		2,600,000		
	£000		*£000*		*£000*
Turnover		13,000		14,300	1,300 F
Expenses:					
Material	2,080		1,950		130 F
Labour	2,340		2,392		52 A
Power	1,690		1,768		78 A
Storage	966		992		26 A
Transport	1,430		1,410		20 F
Maintenance	770		790		20 A
Depreciation	970		960		10 F
Admin expenses	650		658		8 A
Total expenses		10,896		10,920	–
Operating profit		2,104		3,380	1,276 F

By breaking the business down into different expense and income areas, the management information system can enable the business to monitor performance against budget. You will have covered this in some detail in the Professional Diploma Unit Management Accounting: Budgeting.

Looking at the management accounts above, there are variances which management would be likely to investigate, such as the power and material variances as the others seem insignificant.

key performance indicators

The MIS will also be designed to monitor the daily and weekly performance of specific areas of the business which are critical to the business's success. The business may produce quantifiable, or calculated, measures used to evaluate the success of an organisation, employee, etc in meeting an objective for performance. These are known as **key performance indicators (KPIs)** and they will be produced as often as the managers and employees, the internal stakeholders, require them.

For example, a chain of restaurants would have an MIS designed to capture information in the restaurant about types of and spend on meals and drinks, as well as sales per member of waiting staff. This could be via an Electronic Point of Sales System (EPOS), integrated into the accounting system.

The KPIs for this type of business might include:

- Average spend per customer on meals, drinks or both, using the figures from the EPOS and general ledger
- Gross profit margin % by product (eg food and drinks)
- Labour % (Labour spend per shift/ revenue for that shift) X 100
- Daily, weekly and monthly sales for each restaurant, by product (eg food and drinks)

Both the EPOS system and the general ledger will be set up so managers can, by analysis or turnover, drill down into every restaurant by, for example, product or staff member. The information could be used to determine which meals are the most profitable and staff could then be trained to sell these more. Restaurants that have a very low labour %, so sales are being delivered with relatively low labour costs, are being particularly efficient. In restaurants where the labour % is much higher, the managers of those which are more efficient could train these managers how to reduce labour costs, so improving long-term profitability.

As part of Management Accounting: Budgeting, you will have studied standard costing and variance analysis. We will now develop the 'Design for Life' Case Study material introduced in Chapter 1 to remind you of the type of variances that could be used as key performance indicators.

Case Study

DESIGN FOR LIFE LTD: PERFORMANCE INDICATORS

situation

Design for Life Ltd, the example pre-seen material in Chapter 1, has been reviewing its performance and the Finance Director wants to introduce some new performance indicators in the factory to assist in maximising profitability. Design For Life Ltd use standard costing.

Using your knowledge of the business, suggest key performance indicators which might be appropriate for use by the Finance Director, focusing on materials and labour in particular.

solution

As a manufacturing business, making the production process as efficient as possible is essential to maximising profitability. Material costs and labour costs will both be significant, as the furniture is of high quality and finish. As the furniture is produced to set designs, these will have a standard cost set for each one, including a standard cost per metre of wood and standard labour rates for cutting, assembly and finishing, depending on the type of finish.

Materials key performance indicators:

- Material price variance (Actual usage x (standard price per metre – actual price per metre))
- Wastage % ((kg scrapped vs kg used) x 100)

Labour key performance indicators:

- Overtime % ((overtime cost for the period/total production wages for the period) x 100)
- Labour rate variance (actual output x (standard rate – actual rate)) for each department
- Labour efficiency variance (standard labour hours for actual production at standard rate – actual labour hours at standard rate)

Where a business does not use standard costing, the key performance indicators may be more based around sales, contribution and profitability. The MIS system will be designed to ensure this information can be extracted easily. The next Case Study illustrates this.

Case Study

PRETTY POTTERY LIMITED: PERFORMANCE INDICATORS

situation

Pretty Pottery Limited is a small business, based in Ledbury, producing handmade pottery vases for sale in the local area and directly via the internet. It does not currently use standard costing. The following report (on the next page) has been produced, comparing actual results to a flexed budget. The original budget was for 5,000 units and the actual units sold were 6,500.

Flexed Budget Operating Statement 6500 units

	Budget £	Actual £	Variance £
Sales	487,500	495,000	7,500F
Less Variable Costs			
Materials	97,500	112,000	14,500A
Labour	65,000	97,500	32,500A
Production overheads	47,000	55,000	8,000A
Contribution	278,000	230,500	47,500A
Production overheads	25,000	27,000	2,000A
Admin & selling overheads	45,000	51,000	6,000A
Operating profit	208,000	152,500	55,500A

required

Calculate some appropriate performance indicators.

solution

As the business does not use standard costing, the following performance indicators would be appropriate:

Performance indicator	Budget	Actual
Average Sales price per unit	= 487,500/6,500 units = £75.00	= 495,000/6,500 = £76.15
Contribution/Sales ratio	= 278,000/487,500 x 100 = contribution/sales x 100 = 57.0%	= 230,500/495,000 x 100 = 46.6%
Variable cost/sales = total variable costs/total sales x 100	= 209,500/487,500 x 100 = 43.0%	= 264,500/495,000 x 100 = 53.4%
Operating profit % = Operating profit/sales x 100	= 208,000/487,500 x 100 = 42.7%	= 152,500/495,000 x 100 = 30.8%

Pretty Pottery Limited can now see how the operating profit has been eroded by the increased variable costs per unit. This would be an area that the management would seek to monitor more closely in future, perhaps weekly or monthly, to drive up profits, as the variances on labour material and production overhead are significantly out of control. This assumes that the original budget was sound.

changes to MIS as an organisation grows

Often a when a business is set up, it will start using a very simple MIS, perhaps only a simple set of general ledger codes and producing management accounts each month. However, as it grows its information needs will change and so the systems will need to be amended or replaced to enable the business to access the information it needs.

For example, a family that runs one furniture store will need information on weekly sales, type of product sold, wages and monthly management accounts. However, if they decide to open several stores around the country, they would need more information to allow them to budget, monitor and control the different locations. The MIS would need to be able to generate information such as gross profit margin by product, staff costs by department and store and profitability by store so they could run the business and effectively as possible.

financial statements for internal use

Financial statements – and the **ratios** that can be extracted from them – provide management with information about the financial state of the organisation. They will enable the management to analyse past performance and also, in the **master budget**, project future performance.

Areas of particular interest to senior management include:

statement of profit or loss
- sales performance
- gross and net profit margins
- comparison of areas of expense

statement of financial position
- liquidity
- gearing
- return on capital employed

statement of cash flows
- explanation of changes in the cash position of a company
- investments made in assets
- sources of financing

EXTERNAL STAKEHOLDERS AND THEIR INFORMATION NEEDS

The information available to external stakeholders will most commonly be the financial statements. This information may be audited, depending on the size of the business and whether the business or stakeholder believe it to be appropriate. The audit is performed independently of management and gives an opinion as to whether the accounts are accurate and give a true and fair view of the business at the reporting date.

If a small business which falls below audit thresholds is applying for a new bank loan, it is possible the bank will request a set of audited financial statements to support the loan application.

Other information may also be requested. For example:

- **Banks**

  When lending, banks need to assess the financial performance and financial strength of an organisation. They need to make sure that any lending can be repaid and also that there are sufficient assets available for security. They will want to see:

  - a statement of profit or loss to check that profit is being generated
  - a statement of financial position to ensure that a company is not over-geared (ie there is not too much borrowing already in relation to equity)
  - a cash budget to confirm that the company will have adequate cash flow over the next twelve months (note that a 'cash budget' is not the same as a 'statement of cash flows')

- **Suppliers**

  The credit control function of many suppliers requires sight of the accounts of prospective customers – either directly or through credit reference agencies – so that they can carry out ratio analysis before granting credit terms.

- **HM Revenue & Customs**

  The statement of profit or loss will provide the source of the data for the calculation of tax due on profits made.

- **Shareholders and investors**

  The published financial statements of public limited companies contain the statement of profit or loss, statement of financial position and the statement of cash flows. These and the investment ratios they provide enable owners of shares and prospective investors to assess the return they are likely to make on the company shares.

The stakeholder may then use this information to calculate ratios to determine how well the business is performing and how financially stable it is. You have covered ratios in your studies in the Financial Statements of Limited Companies Unit. However, as it is such an important area, the Case Study that follows sets out how to calculate the key ratios which a stakeholder may look at.

TRENDY TOGS LIMITED

situation

Trendy Togs Limited have a unique range of clothing, selling via shops in London, Birmingham, Manchester and Edinburgh. They began to expand rapidly in 20-2 and opened two new shops. They have also started to sell via the internet to other clothes shops and offer 30 days credit. They wish to continue to expand and are looking for additional finance in the form of a bank loan.

Trendy Togs Ltd

Income Statement for the year ended 31 December 20-2

	£000
Revenue	6,528
Cost of sales	3,256
Gross profit	3,272
Administrative	954
Selling and distribution	321
Operating Profit	1,997
Less finance costs	100
Profit before taxation	1,897
Less Taxation	258
Profit after taxation	1,639

Trendy Togs Ltd

Statement of Financial Position as at 31 December 20-2

ASSETS	£000
Non-current assets	16,263
Current assets:	
Inventories	240
Trade receivables	97
Cash and cash equivalents	478
	815
Total assets	17,078
EQUITY AND LIABILITIES	
Equity	
Ordinary share capital (£1 shares)	9,604
Retained earnings	4,862
Total equity	14,466
Non-current liabilities	
Commercial Mortgage	2,000
	2,000
Current liabilities	
Trade payables	354
Tax liabilities	258
	612
Total liabilities	2,612
Total equity and liabilities	17,078

required

(a) Calculate appropriate ratios for the bank to consider.

(b) State with reasons whether you or not you would give them a loan.

solution

(a)

Ratio Analysis

	20-2	Performance indicator 20-2	Workings
Gross margin (Gross profit margin)	50.12%	Gross margin %	Gross profit / revenue * 100 = 3,272/6,528*100 50.12%
Operating margin (Operating profit margin)	30.59%	Operating profit %	Operating profit / revenue *365 = 1,997/6,528*100 30.59%
ROCE (return on capital employed)	12.13%	ROCE %	Operating profit / (Equity + mortgage) * 100 = 1,997/(14,466+2,000)*100 12.13%
Gearing	12.15%	Gearing %	= Loans / (Loans + Equity) x 100 = 2,000/(2,000+14,466) 12.15%
Current ratio (Working capital ratio)	1.33:1	Current ratio	= Current assets / Current liabilities = 815/612 1.33
Acid test (Quick assets test)	0.94:1	Acid test/ Quick ratio	= (Current assets – inventory) / Current liabilities = (815-240)/612 0.94:1
Inventory holding period days	27 days	Inventory holding period	= Inventory / cost of sales * 365 = 240/3,256*365 26.90
Receivables (debtors) collection period (days)	5.4 days	Trade receivables collection period	Trade & other receivables / Revenue * 365 = 97/6,528*365 5.42
Payables (creditors) payment period (days)	39.7 days	Trade payables payment period	Trade payables / cost of sales * = 354/3,256*365 39.68

(b) Trendy Togs Limited has very low gearing at the moment and strong operating and gross profit margins. The current and acid test ratios are reasonable, given the type of industry Trendy Togs Limited operates in.

Given the high profitability, low gearing and good level of liquidity, the bank are likely to give Trendy Togs Limited a loan on good terms.

MAINTAINING RELATIONSHIPS WITH THE STAKEHOLDERS

ethical considerations

Often stakeholders, such as employees, banks, customers and suppliers, enjoy a relationship with an organisation for many years and will request and receive a variety of information over that time.

Any information regarding the company whether it is the weekly sales figures or the year end accounts, must be produced and distributed under ethical principles, by which accountants are bound.

The principle ethical considerations, which you have already studied at Level 3 are set out below.

- **Objectivity** – decisions based on facts, not influenced by other people
- **Integrity** – straightforward and honest dealings with people
- **Professional Behaviour** – complying with the rules and regulations that govern the accounting profession, including upholding the profession's reputation
- **Professional Competence and Due Care** – having the right level of skill, working carefully, thoroughly and to deadlines and declining work when you are not able to perform it
- **Confidentiality** –not disclosing information obtained due to work to third parties

We will now cover these fundamental ethical principles in more detail, along with some practical examples.

objectivity

A person who is objective is a person who sticks to the facts and does not allow his or her decisions or actions to be affected by other people's opinions or influence. Objectivity can be threatened by:

- a conflict of interest – a situation where professional judgement is affected because the employee could benefit personally from a transaction
- undue influence – a situation where someone is putting undue pressure on you to do something that you do not consider professional or ethical

For example, an Assistant Accountant has found out that his immediate boss, the Accounts Manager, takes his wife to Paris on company expenses. The Accounts Manager asks the Assistant Accountant to keep quiet about it, in return for promising to recommend him for promotion.

Similarly, Accounts Payable staff may be asked by the Finance Director to delay supplier payments to improve the cash position of the company at the end of the financial year – this is known as 'window dressing'. This may be against supplier credit terms but, as the Accounts Payable staff report to the Finance Director, they may feel they have to do it, even if it means causing cash flow problems to their suppliers.

integrity

Employees who act with 'integrity' are:

- straightforward – they obey the rules
- honest – they do not cover up the truth, fiddle the books, or allow anything to pass through the accounting system which they know has not been checked
- fair dealing – they treat everyone on an equal basis, they are not involved in 'shady' deals
- truthful – they do not tell lies, falsify or 'fudge' figures, or mislead customers and suppliers with false information, eg prices, discounts

In short, that person will not allow anything that is incorrect or misleading to pass through the accounting system or be given to stakeholders. The principle of integrity applies equally to major and minor breaches of ethics.

For example, if the Chief Accountant was deliberately adjusting sales to avoid paying out bonuses to sales staff at the end of the year, breaching the integrity ethic, the trust built up between the employee and the employer would be harmed. The employees might take legal action against the organisation, they may either leave or behave in a similar way to management, making fraud (covered in Chapter 4) more likely.

If a stakeholder, such as a bank, were to find out information provided to them had been adjusted for any reason, this could result in loan funding being withdrawn. This would have a damaging impact on the long-term future of the business.

professional behaviour

Professional behaviour is the individual complying with the rules and regulations that govern the accounting profession, including upholding the profession's reputation.

The type of rules and regulations might include:

- accounting standards
- the ethical code

Areas where an accountant may damage the profession's reputations are:

- ignoring requests for information or producing information late
- using abusive language with other staff either directly or in emails

For example, the Credit Controller has decided to handle late payers by 'naming and shaming' them on the company website. This behaviour is likely to alienate customers quickly and damage the reputation of the business, as well as the accounting profession.

Similarly, when the Financial Controller knowingly incorrectly records a finance lease as an operating lease, to make the financial statements gearing ratio look better, not only are they acting without integrity, they are also behaving very unprofessionally.

professional competence and due care

Professional Competence means achieving a level of knowledge and skills needed for working at a particular level in the workplace. The more senior the employee, the greater the knowledge and skills that will be needed to perform the work.

Due Care means that the accounting employee must take the required level of care appropriate to the task that is being done. In other words the accounting employee must provide a competent and 'professional' service.

Professional Competence and Due Care require that the accounting employee should:

- act diligently – this means carrying out a task according to instructions, carefully, thoroughly and on time
- use sound judgement in applying professional knowledge
- know when to refuse to carry out an area of work (eg payroll processing) if the employee does not have the necessary knowledge or skills
- plan career progression through CPD (Continuing Professional Development), a programme of qualifications, internal courses and expanding experience

For example, an accounts line manager has been asked to be responsible for the Payroll Section for a few months to cover maternity leave. He has no real experience of this area of the accounting system, but agrees to the request because he is looking for promotion. He is not professionally competent to perform this task.

An Accounts Manager is preparing some financial figures for a company Board Meeting. She is going away on holiday that night, so hurries through the pack and misses updating two key tables. She has not taken due care.

confidentiality

Confidentiality within an Accounting Department is the duty not to disclose information held by the organisation about another person or organisation to anyone else, unless permission has been given.

The type of information that should not be given to outsiders includes personal or business details of:

- customers and clients
- suppliers
- colleagues
- internal information about the organisation

'Outsiders' who should not be given information include:

- family members
- social acquaintances
- 'cold callers', eg marketing survey companies

For example, a Payroll Manager tells his friend, the Accounts Manager, exactly how much the Financial Controller currently earns. The Financial Controller is leaving and the Accounts Manager wants to apply for the position. The Payroll Manager is clearly breaking confidentiality here.

sustainability

As part of your previous studies, you will have considered sustainability, however, to remind you, the definition of sustainability is as follows:

> **'Sustainable development is development that meets the needs of the present without compromising the ability of future generations to meet their own needs.'**

There are three main objectives of sustainability:

- economic growth – decisions are based on the long-term growth of the business
- environmental protection – decisions made do not harm the environment
- social equality – decisions promote the well-being of all employees and the local community

These are sometimes referred to as 'profit, planet and people' and set out below are some examples for each objective.

economic growth

- using fair pricing policies when charging customers
- paying a fair wage, rather than the lowest possible, to allow workers to remain with the business in the long-term and protect its future

environmental protection

- reducing the carbon footprint of a business eg cycle to work schemes, car sharing
- using suppliers who promote sustainable practices in the production of their products

social equality

- sponsorship of local charity events
- employing local labour where possible or training local people to become more skilled and employable

> **Answering the synoptic**
>
> In the synoptic assessment, you will need to ensure you consider sustainability both in terms of areas the business is doing well and also potential improvements it could make to promote more sustainable practices.

Chapter Summary

- There are many different stakeholders who could be interested in a business, both internal and external, including employees and managers, banks, customers, suppliers, the tax authorities.
- The organisation needs to produce information for these stakeholders using a Management Information System (MIS).
- The MIS will be specifically designed to meet the needs of the business in which it operates. For example a retail organisation would collect information on sales by product and location.
- The MIS will provide the business with the right information to allow it to calculate key performance indicators, to assist in running the business and monitoring key areas.
- Within an organisation, budgetary reports and management reports will be created to fit the needs of the managers and employees.
- External stakeholders are likely to be given the financial statements, which they can use for carrying out ratio analysis. This will give an indication of the financial performance and position of the business.
- Accountants are bound by ethics and sustainable principles when providing information to stakeholders. Information provided must comply with those principles and be delivered in a timely and appropriate manner.

Key Terms

stakeholder	a person or organisation that has an 'interest' in another organisation
internal stakeholder	managers and employees who are employed by a business. This could include directors in a large company
external stakeholder	a person or organisation who is connected but not involved in the day to day running of the business, eg banks, customers, suppliers
management Information system	a computer-based system which provides up-to-date, accurate and relevant information to management
key performance indicator	a quantifiable measure used to evaluate the success of an organisation in meeting its objectives for performance
ratio analysis	analysis of the financial statements, often performed by external stakeholders, to evaluate and assess performance and financial stability
ethical principles	the principles by which accountants are bound and under which they must produce accurate, reliable and relevant information
sustainable principles	how a business meets the needs of the present without compromising the ability of future generations to meet their own needs, in terms of economic growth, environmental protection and social equality

Activities

3.1 Speedy Car Services Limited fits tyres, brakes, batteries and exhausts at fifteen branches around the Midlands. They carry many of these items in stock and use one main supplier, who deliveries them daily and can provide more specialist items when needed.

Speedy Car Services Limited have been trading for several years and employ 130 people, most of who have been with the company for several years. The branches operate a bonus system for the employees, based on sales figures for each branch.

Two years ago, the business invested in three new branches as well as improved diagnostic equipment for various makes of car. This investment was funded by a five year loan from the bank. The business is owned by three members of the same family, who all work at one of the main branches.

(a) Identify the key stakeholders of the business, both internal and external and explain why they are important. Give examples of information the stakeholders may wish to look at.

(b) Give examples of some key performance indicators the owners might use to assist in running the business.

3.2 Almost Vintage Limited makes and sells copies of 1950's style vintage clothing to retailers across the globe. They are a well-established business, employing ten people, who use quality fabrics and today's sewing methods to create replica clothing. The business is owned by Narita Stanley.

They have an excellent reputation amongst their customers and many place several orders per year. The usual credit terms offered are 30 days, with some preferred customers being given 45 days. They have very few bad debts.

The fabrics used for the clothing are produced to order in France and Italy by three or four key fabric printers.

(a) Identify the key stakeholders of the business, both internal and external and explain why they are important. Give examples of information the stakeholders may wish to look at.

(b) Give examples of some key performance indicators the business might use.

3.3 Plum Limited manufactures specialist gas detection equipment. The financial statements are set out below:

Statement of profit or loss for the year ended 31 December 20-6

	£000
Revenue	36,000
Cost of Sales	(20,800)
Gross Profit	15,200
Operating expenses	(13,310)
Profit from operations	1,890
Finance costs	(175)
Profit before tax	1,715
Tax	(849)
Profit for the period from continuing operations	866

Statement of Financial Position at 31 December 20-6

ASSETS	*£000*
Non-current assets	
Property, plant and equipment	25,708
	25,708
Current assets	
Inventories	2,736
Trade receivables	3,960
Cash and cash equivalents	757
	7,453
Total assets	33,161
EQUITY AND LIABILITIES	
Equity	
Ordinary share capital (£1 shares)	11,000
Retained earnings	15,950
Total equity	26,950
Non-current liabilities	
Bank loans	3,500
	3,500
Current liabilities	
Trade payables	1,786
Tax liabilities	925
	2,711
Total liabilities	6,211
Total equity and liabilities	33,161

Required:

Calculate relevant key performance indicator ratios to one decimal place. Include ratios to cover profitability, liquidity and financial risk.

3.4 A business may engage in 'window dressing' when producing a set of financial statements. The organisation may delay payments to suppliers and try to speed up credit control. This makes the cash position of the business look better than it normally is and distorts key performance indicators, such as trade receivable collection period and trade payables payment period.

This is an example of what?

(a) Engaging in unethical behaviour	
(b) Engaging in fraudulent behaviour	
(c) Complying with loan terms	
(d) Implementing accounting standards	

3.5 You are the Finance Director for Luxury Cars Limited. Your Managing Director has suggested you use one of the latest, expensive cars to take your family on holiday for a week, as you have 'been doing a great job recently'.

This is an example of what?

(a) A bonus	
(b) Engaging in fraudulent behaviour	
(c) A benefit of working for a luxury car dealership	
(d) Engaging in unethical behaviour	

3.6 You work as the Financial Accountant for a recruitment company. You have one member of staff in your accounts team who would like to study for her AAT but is currently unable to pay for it herself.

By paying for her training, what principle would you be supporting?

(a) Environmental protection	
(b) Objectivity	
(c) Social equality	
(d) Professional behaviour	

3.7 The Accounts Receivable Clerk for Design for Life Ltd, Salam Khan, has been working to resolve several outstanding queries on the account of Furniture World Limited, a very important customer. Aneysha Dickson, Design for Life's Chief Accountant, has suggested to Salam that he visits Furniture World Limited in London, where they are based, to sit down and resolve the queries, face to face. Salam agrees with the suggestion and gets in touch with Mark Brody in Furniture World's Accounts Department. Mark suggests that as Salam has a long distance to travel he might like to stay overnight in London and see a show 'at their expense'.

Required:

(a) Which of Salam's fundamental principles is being threatened by this offer?

(a) Professional behaviour	
(b) Integrity	
(c) Objectivity	

(b) What should Salam do?

(a) Accept and advise Aneysha	
(b) Decline politely	
(c) Decline and report Mark Brody to the AAT for breaking the Code of Ethics	

this chapter covers...

The main part of this chapter explains the internal control systems that are set up in an organisation to implement all the requirements of external regulations and other organisational requirements.

The chapter covers the different types of fraud and how and when they may occur. How to prevent and detect fraud are considered, along with the impact of fraud on the businesses.

The chapter also describes in detail:

- *the purpose of internal control systems*
- *the types of internal controls used in different parts of the accounting system*
- *how the type of internal controls needed are influenced by the type of organisation*
- *the importance of strong internal controls systems to keep the risk of loss, through error or fraud, to a minimum*
- *how ethics and strong internal controls support each other*
- *the usefulness of ratio analysis and key performance indicators (KPIs) in assessing if errors or fraud are occurring*
- *the different types of fraud that can be committed within an organisation*
- *the risk of fraud occurring within an organisation*
- *the areas vulnerable to fraud*
- *the need to design a system so that fraud is minimised, can be easily detected and dealt with as appropriate*
- *the implications for an organisation if fraud occurs*

INTERNAL CONTROL IN AN ACCOUNTING SYSTEM

why do we need internal control systems?

Any accounting system will have certain elements in common, whether it is a company Accounts Department, a Local Authority Purchasing Department or a charitable organisation's fundraising section. It will:

- deal with money – handling cash
- need to make payments and issue cheques
- have 'levels of authority' within the system
- need to make decisions over ordering and purchasing
- need to set budgets for spending
- need to organise its accounting records

Unless the management is happy to let everything become totally disorganised, the accounting system will need to establish various **rules and regulations** which will establish an **internal control system,** for example:

- the establishing of **money limits** for certain transactions
- the definition of **levels of responsibility** for **authorising** transactions
- the need for **referral of decision making** to another person when required

the importance of a robust internal control system

A robust internal control system gives managers confidence that:

- serious errors or missing items in the financial statements are unlikely
- the risk of fraud occurring is as low as possible
- the assets of the business are protected
- liabilities are identified and included correctly in the financial statements
- any financial reports produced are as accurate and up-to-date as possible

This is summarised in the diagram on the next page:

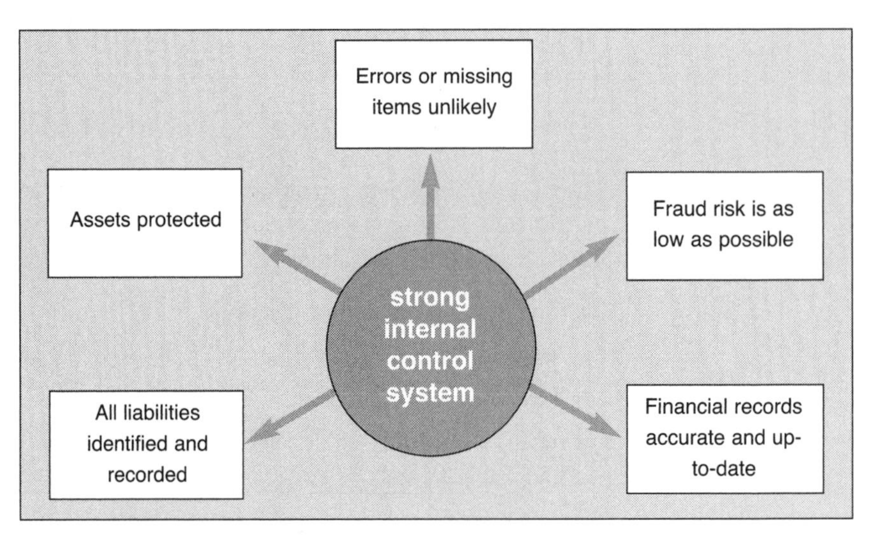

It is important to note that it is the responsibility of senior management to ensure there are strong internal control systems in place.

TYPES OF INTERNAL CONTROL SYSTEMS

Large and medium-sized organisations

Often a medium-sized or large organisation will have policies and procedures in place, which form part of the internal control system.

Illustrated on the next page are extracts from a **Policies and Procedures** internal control document issued by the Accounts and Finance Department of a medium-sized business. Read through this and you will see that there are a number of examples of internal controls. These have been extracted and are shown below.

controls over money limits

All orders of £1,000 or more must be authorised by the budget holder.

All cheques for £1,000 or over require two signatories.

Petty cash will be topped up on the 'imprest' system, where the amount spent is reimbursed. It is intended for small items, up to £20.

controls over authorisation

All invoices must be authorised for payment by the budget holder.

Salary payments require the signature of the Accounts Manager or Financial Controller, plus one other.

referral to another person or higher authority (authorisation controls)

Budget holders will discuss with the Financial Controller appropriate parameters, plus maximum allowed deviations before the budget holder or senior manager is brought in; this will be documented.

Finance must be informed if there are queries delaying authorisation (of payments) or if payment is to be withheld for any reason.

POLICIES AND PROCEDURES STATEMENT– ACCOUNTING AND FINANCE (extracts)

Books of account and records
Proper accounting records will be kept. The accounts systems is based around computer facilities, using Sage and Excel, but manual/paper records will also be used if appropriate. The following records will be kept:

- Appropriate control accounts (bank control, petty cash control, VAT control, salary control)
- Monthly trial balances
- Petty cash and bank accounts will be reconciled at least monthly
- VAT Returns produced on the required quarterly cycle

Ordering supplies and services
Budget holders can place orders for goods or services within their budget areas, subject only to cash-flow restraints. All orders of £1,000 or more must be authorised by the budget holder, except for specific areas of expenditure where written procedures have been agreed. Under £1,000, the budget holder may delegate all ordering as appropriate. Budget holders will discuss with the Financial Controller appropriate parameters, plus maximum allowed deviations before the budget holder or senior manager is brought in, which will be documented.

Payment authorisation and Purchases Ledger
All invoices must be authorised for payment by the budget holder, although the actual checking of details may be delegated. The authorising department is responsible for checking invoices for accuracy in terms of figures and conformity with the order placed, that the services or goods have been received, and following up any problems. Finance must be informed if there are queries delaying authorisation or if payment is to be withheld for any reason.

A Purchases Ledger is operated by Finance. All incoming invoices are to be passed to Finance section as soon as they arrive. Invoices will be recorded in the Purchases Ledger within two days, unless there are coding problems. They are then passed on to budget holders for authorisation. Once authorised as above, suppliers will be paid within the appropriate timescale.

Cheque writing and signing
Signatories will only be drawn from senior staff and directors, and any new signatory must be approved by the directors before the bank is notified. All cheques for £1,000 or over require two signatories. Cheque signatories should check that the expenditure has been authorised by the appropriate person before signing the cheque. Salary payments require the signature of the Accounts Manager or Financial Controller, plus one other. Cheques should be filled in completely (with payee, amount in words and figures, and date) before cheques are signed.

Handling of cash
Petty cash will be topped up on the 'imprest' system, where the amount spent is reimbursed. It is intended for small items, up to £20. Anything over this should be paid by cheque where possible. The imprest has a balance limit of £250. The petty cash balance will be reconciled when re-storing the imprest balance, or monthly if this is more frequent. All cash collected from Finance will be signed for, and receipts will be issued for all cash returned.

As you can see, an internal control system is made up a variety of individual controls over different elements of the purchasing process. We will consider the specific type of controls a business could put in place in particular accounting systems in the next chapter, when we consider what makes an effective accounting system.

small organisations

A smaller organisation may have different accounting control systems, where the emphasis is more on key individuals using authorisation and management review controls, rather than written policies and procedures.

For example in a small owner-managed business, there may only be one or two members of accounts staff. The accounts will be produced by this small team who are aware of the trading performance of the business and are likely to identify fraud or errors as and when they arise.

The owner will also be aware of most of the business' transactions, as they are probably going to be significantly involved with buying and selling items. As the owner is likely to be the main signatory, they will probably review all the payments as they are made, and ask about anything they do not know about or do not understand, so errors or fraud by the accounts staff are less likely to happen. Similarly, the owner may track the sales figures and compare this to the management accounts, produced periodically, and investigate the difference themselves. This review process is likely to identify any errors or items which are missing – a strong internal control system.

However, with this type of system, there is little **segregation** of duties (see page 77) and the owner needs to be particularly aware of this, and watch carefully for potential fraud.

types of internal controls

The internal control system relies on several different types of controls to operate in all areas of the accounting systems. When we go on to look at effective accounting systems in the next chapter, we will review the controls we expect to see in systems such as payroll, sales and purchasing. For now, you can see on the following page, the type of controls which are commonly found in accounting systems:

Type of Control	Example
Segregation	The Accounts Receivable Clerk, who enters invoices, cannot receive and record cash receipts
Organisation	Clear, defined roles for staff in appropriate departments, eg Finance, Production, Human Resources
Authorisation	Credit notes over £2,000 need to be authorised by the Finance Director
Physical	Petty cash tin a kept in a locked drawer
Supervision	The Management Accountant supervises the Accounts Payable Clerk to ensure duties are carried out to the required standard
Personnel	Qualified, competent staff
Arithmetical and Accounting	The wages control account is reconciled regularly
Management	Management accounts are produced and reviewed each month, with variances investigated

THE USE OF KPIS AND RATIOS

A company needs strong internal controls to ensure it is producing the most accurate reliable information. However, if weaknesses exist, how might management become aware of this? The answer is comparing information with historic data and when it is different, investigating why the differences occur. There are two main types of data that management can consider:

- key performance indicators
- ratios

key performance indicators

In Chapter 3 we considered the type of key performance indicators our business, Design For Life Ltd might use. We will now look in a Case Study at how this information might suggest errors or fraud may be taking place.

Case Study

DESIGN FOR LIFE LTD: KEY PERFORMANCE INDICATORS

situation

The business monitors production by product type, using KPIs. The table for two of the KPIs is shown below:

Key performance indicator	Period 10 (4 weeks)	Period 9 (4 weeks)	Yearly average
Oak dining table – Iago			
Material Wastage % (kg scrapped vs kg used)x100	3%	2.0%	2.0%
Reject rate %	1.5%	0.2%	0.2%
Overtime % (overtime cost per period/total production wages for the period) x 100	15%	5%	8%

The material wastage % is 50% higher in period 10 than period 9 and above the yearly average. This could be due to a change in materials and quality, but if the workforce and materials supplier were the same in each period, wastage could have increased due to wood being scrapped unnecessarily and taken off site and sold. Alternatively there may be a problem with inventory bookings and not all wood is being recorded correctly against the Iago job. The wastage would appear high, as total kg used would be lower than expected. In the long-term, this could mean jobs are not being costed correctly and prices may be too low to recover all costs and make a profit. Both of these could arise due to weaknesses in controls over inventory and wastage.

The reject rate is also very high in period 10. If there are not sufficient physical controls in place to control rejects, inventory and movements in and out of the factory tables could be being fraudulently recorded as rejected, then taken from the factory and sold to a third party.

The overtime % is three times higher in period 10 than period 9. This could be due to a problem with the recording of overtime, which is being overpaid. This might be due to an error in the overtime rates being used, where the rate is too high, or a problem with the recording of time on timesheets or through the clocking in system. Both of these could mean overtime is being paid unnecessarily.

ratios

Ratio analysis may also indicate areas in the accounts where controls may not be operating effectively. The Case Study below highlights this.

Case Study

CARABEN'S COSTUME HIRE LTD

situation

Cara and her brother, Ben, run a costume hire business in Oxford. They supply theatres and TV production companies across the UK with period costumes. They offer regular customers 30 days credit, although sometimes offer cash terms to new businesses. They employ 10 staff, including one bookkeeper, who also runs the payroll and undertakes Credit Control.

They have just been given the following information by their accountant, based on draft figures, who suggested Caraben need to review their current accounting procedures, as he believes there could be serious weaknesses in the sales system.

	This year - draft	**Last year**
Gross Profit margin %	45%	55%
Accounts Receivable Collection Period	60 days	35 days

required

Review the ratios and consider what type of weaknesses could exist in Caraben's systems this year.

solution

Gross profit margin %
The gross profit margin % is significantly lower this year than last year. This could mean that sales are not being correctly recorded. Cash sales may not be recorded correctly or the sales invoicing process may not be operating correctly, so credit customers are not being charged for every hire. Alternatively, the cost of sales figure could be too high, if items have been posted there incorrectly. Finally, they may have not passed on cost increases to their customers in the hire charges.

Accounts receivable collection period
The accounts receivable collection period has almost doubled. This could be linked to the lack of recording of sales, as fewer sales would make the year-end balance a larger proportion of the total. Alternatively, the credit control system may not be operating correctly when chasing up old customers, so debts remain outstanding for longer.

the impact of ethics

The directors of a company and senior management will determine the culture of the organisation, which affects the environment in which the accounting system operates. If the directors behave ethically, employees are more likely to do this as well. Conversely, if the directors behave unethically, staff may believe this is acceptable. This could result in more instances of fraud and error, by both the directors and staff.

For example, Volkswagen is known to have misstated results for CO_2 emissions tests on its cars, so customers were misinformed when they purchased them. This was done knowingly by employees and is estimated to have cost Volkswagen Euro 6.8 billion. Had strong internal control systems been in place and the ethical standards been clear, this may not have happened at all.

An ethical company is likely to have strong internal control systems if it has following characteristics:

- clear communication of the ethical values of the business, putting integrity at the heart of dealing with everyone
- competent, qualified staff who are committed to their work and ensure they perform it to a high standard
- directors and managers who behave professionally, ensuring they follow relevant rules and regulations which apply
- decisions being made in an objective, unbiased manner, such as authorisation according to set limits

reviewing the accounting system

In the synoptic assessment, you will be required to review an accounting system. You will need to appreciate that if an accounting system has weaknesses it will be because the internal control system will be deficient in one way or another. This will lead to various possible problems:

- **errors being made** because people do not know the correct way of doing things
- errors being made **and not being picked up** because the processes are not being checked properly
- **fraud being committed** because the internal control system is deficient and the opportunity for fraud is there for the taking

Answering the synoptic assessment

As part of the synoptic assessment, you will be asked to evaluate an accounting system. You will have been given pre-release material, to help you think about the type of internal controls that might be suitable for that business. You will need to consider whether the business behaves ethically and whether there are likely to be strong or weak internal control systems.

TYPES OF FRAUD

Fraud is an unfortunate fact of life within organisations. It sometimes hits the headlines, as when a merchant banker's PA diverted over £1 million of her employer's funds into designer clothes, cars, speedboats, and general high living. This is obviously an extreme example which makes good material for the media, but the principle involved is the same as the employee who walks off with the employer's stationery or petty cash, or who sneaks out of work an hour early to watch a football match.

Fraud within an organisation can therefore be described as an activity which presents a threat of some form of loss to the employer:

- **loss of money**, eg theft of petty cash
- **loss of inventory**, eg theft of products by supermarket staff
- **loss of time**, eg disappearing from work to do something else during contracted work hours

It is the responsibility of the management of an organisation to:

- identify areas where the **risk of fraud** exists and to grade the seriousness of the risk in each case
- set up **control systems** involving all staff to alert management to possible occurrence of fraud
- monitor those control systems on a regular basis to ensure that they are working
- deal with any incidence of fraud in an appropriate way, whether it be a formal warning or calling in the police

It is important to define in more detail what we mean by 'fraud', and we will consider this next.

some definitions

Fraud covers a variety of offences, but a general definition of fraud is:

the use of deception with the intention of obtaining an advantage, avoiding an obligation or causing loss to someone else or to an organisation

Fraud is a criminal activity and is covered in the UK by a number of laws:

theft	dishonestly taking someone else's property (Theft Act)
false accounting	dishonestly destroying, defacing, concealing or falsifying an accounting record for personal gain or to cause loss to someone else (Theft Act)
bribery and corruption	taking or giving a bribe that might influence the actions of others (Prevention of Corrupt Practices Acts and Bribery Act 2010)
deception	obtaining property, money, services or evading liability by deception (Theft Act)

practical examples of fraud

In practical terms fraud is normally a combination of any of the following:

- theft of property or money or information (eg someone copying and selling the company's customer database to a competitor)
- falsification of records so that property or money is passed to the wrong person (eg someone 'fiddling' the payroll)
- collusion – ie a 'set-up' between an employee and someone else outside the organisation, eg false invoices sent in by an outsider for supplies that were never made and authorised and paid by the person 'on the inside'

public examples of fraud

There are many examples of fraud which are made public. Students involved in the public sector would find it useful to investigate the HM Treasury Fraud Reports, available as downloads from the website www.hm-treasury.gov.uk. These contain examples of fraud in local authorities and Government departments. Types of fraud in the private sector are very similar. The examples on the next page have been adapted from cases reported by a leading insurance company.

REPORTED CASES OF FRAUD

Theft of fuel stocks – *Total Loss £25,000*

A local authority had their own fuel pumps for supplying their motor vehicles. The employee in charge stole fuel over a long period as the inventory checks were inadequate.

Payroll fraud: fictitious employees – *Total Loss £10,000*

The manager of an industrial cleaning company invented bogus employees, put them on the payroll and then cashed their pay cheques.

Bank deposits: teeming and lading – *In 10 months a total of £7,000 was stolen.*

A clerk in charge of a sub post office stole cash receipts due to be paid into the local bank. This was covered up by delaying paying in at the bank and altering the paying-in slips relating to subsequent deposits. Stealing money received from one source and then using money received from other sources to cover it up is known as 'teeming and lading'.

Cheque printing machine – *Total Loss £25,000*

A ledger clerk responsible for making regular payment of rent for advertising was in charge of a machine that printed cheques. Numerous small cheques were made out by him for the correct amounts but payable to him. It was several months before complaints from creditors, (who had not received their cheques) were investigated and the fraud uncovered.

Collusion: stock control system – *Total Loss £1 million*

A well known national company was defrauded by two gangs of employees working at the same location. The losses involved collusion between warehousemen and drivers who used the spare capacity on vehicles to remove goods from the depot. False information was entered into the computerised inventory control system and their activities were only discovered when the police reported finding large amounts of the particular product in the hands of third parties.

Collusion: fictitious sub-contractors – *Total Loss exceeded £500,000*

A major contractor with well established control systems to approve payments were the victims of fraud by a section supervisor in collusion with a computer operator. Cheques were made out to fictitious sub-contractors and despatched to private addresses.

RISK ASSESSMENT AND FRAUD

risk assessment – the role of management

Assessment of **fraud risk** is part of the **risk assessment** process which is the responsibility of organisations in both the private and the public sectors.

In the case of limited companies (private sector), the Turnbull Report has stated that directors have responsibility for ensuring that risk management practices are established as part of an effective internal control system.

In the public sector the guiding document to fraud risk is HM Treasury's 'Managing the Risk of Fraud – a Guide for Managers' available as a download from www.hm-treasury.gov.uk

The assessment of risk generally by management follows a number of distinct stages. This process applies equally to the assessment of fraud risk:

- setting up a risk management group and identifying objectives
- identifying the areas of risk of fraud
- grading the scale of the risk in each case
- developing a strategy to manage that risk
- setting up systems to detect and deal with fraud, allocating responsibility
- getting the systems up and running
- monitoring the running of the system

the internal control system– fraud prevention

A robust internal control system is essential if management is going to be able to detect and deal with fraud.

There are various techniques that can be used for making an internal control system 'fraud resistant':

- **fraud staff**
  Some very large organisations may appoint employees – eg ex-bank or ex-police staff – to work full-time on fraud prevention and detection.

- **management responsibility**
  Managers should be given specific areas of responsibility and answerability – eg sections of the Accounts Department – to ensure that fraud is kept to a minimum.

- **management supervision**
  Management – particularly line management – should supervise accounting activities on a regular basis. This involves overseeing and checking activities such as data entry to computers, making payments and payroll processing.

- **segregation of duties**
  The system should be set up so that duties which, when combined, could lead to fraud, are given to different people – ie they are segregated. For example, the cashier taking in cash for a business should ideally not be the same person who makes out the paying-in slip for the bank. The danger is that some of the cash may disappear into the cashier's pocket.

- **lock & key**
  Physical security – locking valuable items away – is a sure deterrent to theft. This does not only apply to cash: the tendency of items such as laptop computers and mobile phones to disappear has become a well-known and ever-increasing statistic.

- **authorisation**
  Some accounting activities may require authorisation by a nominated official. This ranges from the authorisation of petty cash, signing of cheques over a certain amount to the investing of liquid funds, eg placing £250,000 on a money market account. Clearly the larger the amount, the more senior the person giving authorisation.

detecting fraud

We have already seen the various areas in which fraud can occur. Fraud can be detected by the experienced manager by simple observation and through experience. Some of the tell-tale and danger signs include:

- employees acting suspiciously – looking shifty and hiding paperwork
- employees with higher levels of spending than you would expect from their income – the payroll clerk who has a new Porsche
- employees working long hours and taking less than the normal holiday entitlement – it is often when employees are away that other employees notice suspicious signs and uncover criminal activity
- employees who have a grudge against the organisation – they may have been passed over for promotion or they may even have a political or ethical axe to grind
- employees who are known to be short of money – they may be struggling with a high mortgage or may even have a drugs problem

grading likelihood and impact

Part of the process of the management of fraud risk is the decision about whether a risk is a **likely** one or not. The likelihood of risk can be divided into three levels:

- **high** – the likelihood of fraud is at a high level (disappearing biros)
- **medium** – the likelihood is possible (theft of cash, collusion)
- **low** – the likelihood is remote (removal of assets from a company pension fund)

The risk of fraud occurring can also be given a **numerical value**: for example a range of 1 to 5, where the higher the risk the higher the number.

Risk assessment also needs to decide whether the **impact** of the fraud is significant. Impact can relate to the **financial state** of the organisation. A major loss through fraud could seriously affect profit and liquidity. For example, the fraudulent trading by an employee of Barings Bank led to its collapse. The fraud can also seriously affect employees, as in the Robert Maxwell case in which employees' pensions were appropriated by the Chairman and Chief Executive.

Generally speaking, frauds that are likely (the disappearing biro) have a lower impact than the remote risk (removal of assets from a company pension fund). The **impact** of a fraud can therefore be similarly graded:

- **high** – the effects of fraud are very serious for the organisation, affecting its profit and/or liquidity
- **medium** – the effects of the fraud are significant but can be dealt with internally, or in some cases by the police (theft, collusion)
- **low** – the impact of the fraud is insignificant (petty pilfering)

using a matrix to grade fraud risk

Organisations sometimes use a matrix to assess the extent of fraud risk in an accounting system. The areas of the system in which the fraud might occur must first be identified, for example:

- cash payments
- cash receipts
- sales ledger
- purchases ledger
- expenses
- inventory control
- payroll
- fixed asset purchase

A matrix (or a section of a matrix) will then be drawn up for each of the areas identified. An example of entries in a typical matrix is illustrated below. The matrix might display:

- the identified risk area of the organisation
- the details of the type of fraud
- the role of the employee who may become involved in it
- any third party who may become involved through collusion
- the likelihood of the fraud (high, moderate, low)
- the impact of the fraud (high, moderate, low)
- action to take to prevent the fraud

This matrix will then become a valuable tool which will enable management to assess the risks and establish an appropriate strategy for minimising them. Note that the format of the matrices you will encounter in your studies may vary. The example below is fairly typical and could be used in your Report.

accounting system fraud matrix – some sample entries

Details of Risk	Employees	Collusion	Likelihood	Impact	Action to take
Payroll section: Stationery pilferage	payroll staff	none	high	low	Lock cabinet. One person controls access
Theft of cash	payroll staff	none	medium	medium	Two people assemble cash pay packets
Payments to fictitious employees	payroll staff	third party recipients	medium	medium	Review of payroll. BACS authorisation by Finance Director and one other
Purchase ledger: Paying fictitious suppliers	buyer	third party recipients	medium	medium	Only Purchasing Manager can access supplier master files to set up new suppliers and their bank details
etc . . . etc . . .					

Answering the synoptic assessment

As part of the synoptic assessment, you may be asked to identify potential frauds and evaluate the likelihood of fraud in the business and consider what you do to prevent it from happening in the future. As you become more familiar with effective systems and the controls you expect to see in accounting systems, in Chapter 5, you can then see when controls are missing and hence where the opportunity for fraud may exist.

THE IMPACT OF FRAUD

financial impact

When fraud occurs, a business may suffer financial loss. How significant the financial impact is often depends on how large the fraud is.

For example, a person stealing from petty cash each week will be committing a serious but low value fraud, which is unlikely to cause the business significant harm in the long-term. However, the employees who misreported the data for Volkswagen, and committed the fraud, have already had a significant financial impact on the business. The company has provided €6.8 billion to cover expected costs relating to the fraud, which is equal to the entire operating profit for 2014. Volkswagen has the reserves to deal with such a large claim. However, a business with less financial strength could cease to operate if the financial loss is very significant.

non-financial impact

The financial impact of a fraud can often be measured reliably. However, the non-financial impact can be just as great but be harder to quantify. There may be damage to employee relations or reputation in the industry.

Volkswagen, for example, has misled customers, who may now no longer believe they can trust the business. This may stop them buying Volkswagen cars in the future and this lack of future sales will be very hard to measure. Current employees may feel that they no longer wish to work for Volkswagen and leave. Potential employees who could add value to Volkswagen's business may decide to work for another car company in preference. The damage to Volkswagen's reputation is impossible to measure and may affect their business for years ahead.

As you will have gathered from this chapter, fraud is inevitable. The lesson for the organisation is – be prepared.

some useful websites

- www.sfo.gov.uk
- www.icaew.com
- www.hm-treasury.gov.uk

In order to access information about fraud you are likely to have to carry out a website search on 'fraud'.

This chapter concludes with two Case Studies on fraud and analysis of fraud published by HM Treasury. They should provide you with an understanding of how a weakness in the accounting system can make fraud possible.

Case Study

TRAVEL AND SUBSISTENCE FRAUD

situation

This fraud involved an employee who travelled regularly on official business. He set his own programme of visits which was not checked by his manager. He then regularly submitted fraudulent travel and subsistence claims which included examples of:

- Claiming subsistence allowances in excess of entitlement.
- Claiming for overnight stays in hotels when in fact he had stayed with friends or family.
- Claiming for visits not made.
- Forging authorising signatures.
- Inflating claims by altering details on claim forms after authorisation by countersigning officer.

These claims were paid by the finance team despite the lack of receipts, invoices or other supporting documents to verify his expenditure. Travel and subsistence guidance was also out-of-date and consequently had fallen into disuse.

The fraud came to light when his office tried to contact him at a hotel where he claimed to be staying. An investigation uncovered a large number of fraudulent claims spanning several years and the employee was eventually prosecuted.

required

Identify the control weaknesses in the expenses system which allowed the fraud to take place.

solution

- Inadequate guidance on submitting, authorising and paying claims.
- Inadequate supervision by line management.
- Failure of countersigning officer to verify that journeys had been made.
- Inadequate control exercised by countersigning officer in returning signed claim forms to the claimant rather than passing them directly to finance team.
- Inadequate checks by finance teams to query amendments to claims, verify countersignatures and ensure that receipts and invoices were included to substantiate claims.
- Absence of spot-checks on claims by the finance team management.

Case Study

CASH HANDLING FRAUD

situation

Transactions involving receipts of cash or cheques are high risks. Of the cases of staff fraud reported to the Treasury each year, a significant proportion involves misappropriation of cash. In this Case Study, a member of staff committed a number of frauds over a period of five years, resulting in a loss of over £10,000.

The organisation's business included the receipt of cheques through the post and cash cheques over the counter. It was the responsibility of the member of staff to receive, record and prepare the receipts for banking. She had been in the job several years and her line managers, who trusted her implicitly, had given her sole responsibility for these duties. They were no longer carrying out checks or monitoring the process.

She would arrive early each morning, usually before her colleagues, and open the post on her own. Money handed in over the counters was also passed to her for banking. However, she did not record or account for the cheques or money prior to banking. She would however, complete a daily cash balance record as part of the banking reconciliation procedures, but by this time she had already removed some of the cash and a number of cheques. There were no independent cross-checks between the documentation which came with the receipts and the amounts sent for banking. To make matters worse, written procedures were out-of-date and had fallen into disuse.

The fraud came to light during the employee's infrequent absences on leave. A minor query by a member of the public regarding a previous payment led to an unexplained difference between the amount quoted in the documentation accompanying the payment and the amount recorded by the employee and banked.

Internal audit were brought in to carry out an initial investigation. They identified major discrepancies between records of receipts kept by counter staff, documentation accompanying payments from members of the public and the amounts being banked. The police were called in and under questioning the officer admitted the offences. She had opened a bank account with the initials of the organisation and had been paying in cash and cheques over a five year period. The case was taken to court and on conviction she was given a custodial sentence and had to repay the amount stolen.

required

Identify the control weaknesses in the cash receipts and banking system which allowed the fraud to take place.

solution

- Lack of separation of duties between post opening, preparation of cash and cheques for banking and reconciliation of amounts banked.
- Inadequate supervision and monitoring by line management.
- Absence of management checks of accounting records, cash balances or bank reconciliations.
- Over-reliance on the honesty and integrity of one individual.
- Lack of adequate written instructions.
- Unawareness of implications of reluctance to use leave entitlement.
- The internal audit report also identified organisational factors which had contributed to the fraud. The main ones were:
  - the organisation had not assessed the risk of fraud
  - there was no policy statement on fraud
  - line managers were not clear about their responsibilities
  - manuals and procedures were poorly structured and out-of-date

Chapter Summary

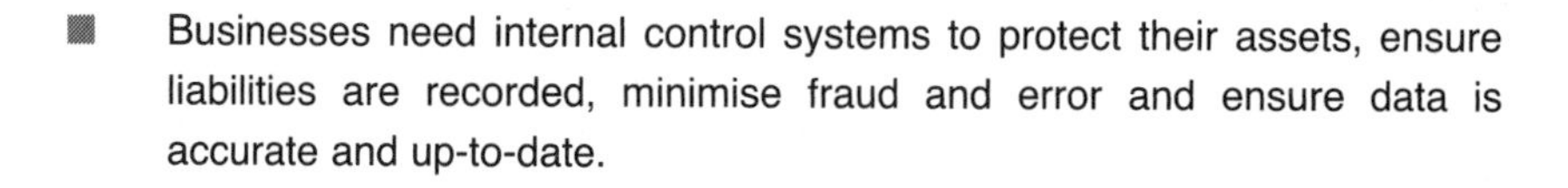

- Businesses need internal control systems to protect their assets, ensure liabilities are recorded, minimise fraud and error and ensure data is accurate and up-to-date.
- Internal controls are individual activities that form part of the internal control system, such as authorisation and qualified personnel.
- Large organisations may have policies and procedures written down for staff to comply with, as part of their internal control system.
- Small organisations will rely on senior management review and authorisation by owners/directors to minimise fraud and error in the business.
- Weaknesses within accounting systems may be highlighted by changes in key performance indicators, including key ratios.
- A strong internal controls system will be supported by strong ethical values in an organisation.
- Types of fraud include theft, false accounting or reporting, bribery and deception. Sometimes fraud involves collusion, where two people work together to commit fraud.
- The directors of the business are required to protect the business against fraud and error. They must put controls in place to do this.
- A business may review its policies and procedures to identify the areas where fraud is most likely and to consider the impact of fraud on it. They may grade the likelihood and impact, either using High, Medium or Low or a grading system 1 to 5, where the higher the number the greater the risk.
- The impact of fraud can be financial, in the form of lost income or assets. There can also be non-financial impacts, such as loss of reputation and custom in the future. Employees may leave or refuse to join such a business.

Key Terms

internal control	a process put in place by management to prevent or detect fraud or errors eg authorisation, segregation
internal control system	the rules and regulations, including internal controls, in place in an accounting system eg payroll to detect and prevent fraud and error
segregation of duties	the separation of the responsibility for the recording of a financial transaction (eg a sale) and the responsibility for the recording of its settlement (ie the customer paying)
policies and procedures	internal documents issued by the Finance Department stating how accounting items should be dealt with by the business eg Purchases and payments, Sales and Credit Control
fraud	the use of deception with the intention of obtaining an advantage, avoiding an obligation or causing loss to someone else or to an organisation
fraud grading assessment	the process where a potential fraud is given a grade – High, Medium or Low or 1 to 5 (5 being the most likely) – of it occurring

Activities

4.1 Who is responsible for ensuring the accounting systems and controls are designed to prevent and detect fraud? Tick the appropriate options below.

(a) The Finance Director	
(b) The Managing Director	
(c) The Human Resources Director	
(d) All of the above	

4.2 List the common types of fraud.

4.3 Explain what segregation of duties is and how it prevents fraud, giving an example.

4.4 Gino Giardino runs Giardino Services Ltd, a successful gardening business, providing garden maintenance services to customers, both business premises and private households. He employs five people and provides them each with garden equipment and a small van. Their main job involves cutting and maintaining lawns and hedging on a fixed contract with each customer. The same people look after the same customers each month. Each gardener completes a weekly timesheet stating how long they have spent at each customer's house or premises. Gino pays them a fixed hourly rate, based on this timesheet.

Periodically, customers will request one-off jobs to be done, such as pruning and weeding whilst the gardener is there. These are done on a cash basis and each employee is given an invoice book, in which to record the sale. They put the cash in their cash tin and return the tin and invoice book to Gino once a week. He banks the receipts and uses his bank statement to update sales.

Required:

(a) Identify and explain two possible frauds which could occur.

(b) Grade the risk and impact on the business of each fraud, using the grading system High, Moderate or Low.

(c) For each fraud, identify one action Gino could take to reduce the risk of the fraud happening.

4.5 Cook Right Limited is a small chain of three shops, specialising in the selling kitchen and cooking equipment, all of which have been trading for several years. The accountant recently produced the financial statements for the year and is concerned that key ratios are worse this year compared to last year. The accountant suspects there may be some problems with the accounting systems in place, so items are not being recorded or are being recorded incorrectly.

The income statement and statement of financial position are set out below and on the next page, along with some key ratios.

Income statement	**This year** *£000*	**Last year** *£000*
Continuing operations		
Revenue	1,200	1,300
Cost of sales	(820)	(780)
Gross profit	380	520
Distribution costs	(130)	(160)
Administrative expenses	(45)	(60)
Profit from operations	205	300
Finance costs	(12)	(10)
Profit before tax	193	290
Tax	(58)	(75)
Profit for the year from continuing operations	135	215

Statement of Financial Position	This year *£000*	Last year *£000*
Assets		
Non –current assets	131	105
Current assets		
Inventories	271	195
Trade receivables	148	125
Cash and cash equivalents	25	63
	444	383
Total assets	575	488
Equity and liabilities		
Equity		
Share capital	10	10
Retained earnings	348	267
Total equity	358	277
Non-current liabilities		
Bank loan	30	33
	30	33
Current liabilities		
Trade payables	124	96
Tax liability	63	82
	187	178
Total liabilities	217	211
Total equity and liabilities	575	488

Ratio	This year *£000*	Last year *£000*
Gross profit percentage margin %	32%	40%
Operating profit margin %	17%	23%
Distribution costs / revenue x 100 %	11%	12%
Inventory days	121 days	91 days
Trade receivable collection days	45 days	35 days

Required

Using the information above, suggest possible reasons for the changes in the financial statements due to problems with the accounting systems in the business.

4.6 Prove It Limited is a successful bakery, with a shop in Burton, selling bread and cakes made on the premises. It employs two full-time bakers and four serving staff. Two of the serving staff work Saturdays. The Manager, is employed full-time and the last member of serving staff works in the mornings until 1.00pm, unless the shop is particularly busy, in which case the Manager authorises additional hours.

The bakers review the previous week's sales, to decide how much to make of each type of bread or cake. The Manager is responsible for valuing any inventory at the end of the day, which will have to be thrown away as waste.

The owner, Nina Bollywood, has been looking over the last period's set of results, set out below, and is concerned that the internal controls in the bakery have not been working properly:

Key performance indicator	This period	Last period
Labour % (Labour cost /revenue x 100)	35%	25%
Value of waste bread or cake (unsold) / Revenue x 100	5%	2%
Average Sales Value per day (till reading)	£300	£400

Required:

Identify the main controls which may have failed to operate and explain how they have impacted on the key performance indicators.

4.7 Lift Express Limited undertook a review of their activities recently and identified the following potential frauds. There are no controls currently in place to prevent them. Complete the grading table and a possible action to prevent and/or detect the possible fraud.

Details of Risk	Employees	Collusion	Likelihood	*Impact & Grade (5-1)	Possible control
IT Theft of customer pricing due to open access to files	Accounts, IT	None			
Payroll Wages payments overstated on timesheets	Production hourly paid	None			
Warehouse Taking inventory for own use or selling on	Stores, Production	Third party recipients			

*Grade either high, medium or low or use numerical system 1-5 where 5 is the highest rating

this chapter covers...

In this chapter we will look at the type of accounting systems in place for different areas of the business, looking at the internal controls within them, and how those integrated systems meet the information needs of the business.

The accounting systems being explained are:

- *purchases and cash payments*
- *revenue and cash receipts*
- *payroll*
- *costing and inventory*
- *capital expenditure*

We will then consider how an effective, integrated accounting system can supply information the business needs to operate efficiently, including an accurate and detailed general ledger.

We will finally consider how effective systems can support ethical and sustainable practices.

WHY ARE EFFECTIVE SYSTEMS IMPORTANT?

A business needs to know that all transactions that it enters into are recorded accurately and reliably. For example:

- all cash sales are recorded
- credit sales are recorded so money can be collected from customers
- business purchases are recorded and suppliers paid for the goods
- capital items are only purchased when the business needs to buy them and they have been authorised correctly
- staff are paid for the hours they work and at the right rate
- the general ledger accurately reflects how money has been earned and spent, so that decisions made on information in the ledger are valid
- the financial statements are an accurate, reliable reflection of the financial performance, as well as the assets, liabilities and equity of the business

Without this accurate information, many issues could arise:

- sales may not be recorded or collected, reducing the business's profitability
- purchases could be made for individuals through the business, not for it, so fraud could occur, as people might believe the business will not notice
- the directors could make decisions regarding pricing, which are made on costing information containing errors or being out of date. If they consequently price products too low, the business could fail to cover all its costs and make a loss, potentially putting it out of business
- capital items could be purchased unnecessarily, incurring additional costs
- staff could be overpaid for work they have not performed again reducing the profitability of the business
- decisions made on the basis of management accounts, produced from the general ledger, may not be based on accurate, reliable information

requirements of an effective system

An effective accounting system should ensure that the transactions within it are recorded:

- completely – all revenue and expenses are included
- for the sole purpose of the business – no personal items are included
- accurately – at the right value
- in the right period – only revenue or expenses that have arisen in this year, should be recorded in this year
- in the right account – it is recorded either in the right nominal ledger account or in the correct supplier or customer account

Answering the synoptic assessment

You will be asked in the synoptic assessment to review an accounting system and identify where controls may be missing or where there is potential for people to commit fraud ie weaknesses within it. Unless you have worked in this part of the business, accounts receivable, for example, this can be difficult to do. To help you, most of this chapter looks at each accounting system and considers what constitutes a good system. This is important for the next chapter which covers the evaluation and review of these systems, which are also tested in the synoptic assessment.

a short recap – internal controls

For any accounting system to be effective, there needs to be controls within it, to prevent and detect fraud and errors. We looked at this in the previous chapter and the main types of controls are summarised below, along with an example for each:

Type of control	Example
Segregation	The Accounts Receivable Clerk, who enters invoices, cannot receive and record cash receipts
Organisation	Clear, defined roles for staff in appropriate departments, eg Finance, Production, Human Resources
Authorisation	Credit notes over £2,000 need to be authorised by the Finance Director
Physical	Petty cash tin a kept in a locked drawer
Supervision	The Management Accountant supervises the Accounts Payable Clerk to ensure duties are carried out to the required standard
Personnel	Qualified, competent staff
Arithmetical and Accounting	The wages control account is reconciled regularly
Management	Management accounts are produced and reviewed each month, with variances investigated

We are now going to consider each accounting system in turn looking at:

- the elements of the system, stating what happens within it
- the requirements of the system for it to be effective

- the controls in place in an effective system, including the information required for it to operate
- potential errors that could occur if adequate controls are not in place

THE PURCHASES AND CASH PAYMENTS SYSTEM

system elements

The diagram below shows the elements of a basic purchases system. (Note that *internal controls* are shown in italics.)

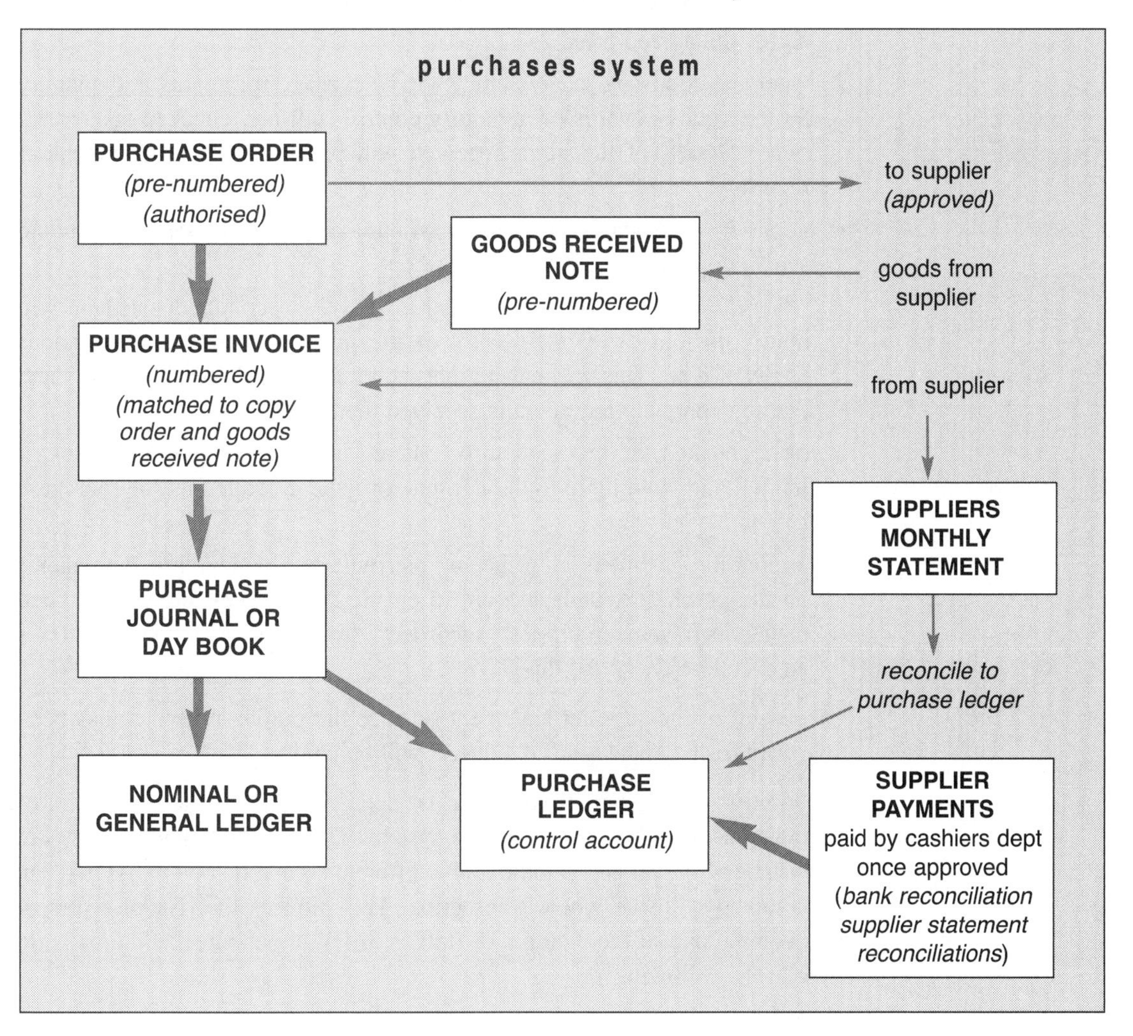

Within this system there are several internal controls. The system works broadly as follows:

- the purchase order will be raised by the buying department. It should be authorised by someone who has the authority to purchase goods or services on behalf of the company and it must be within their authorisation limit. It may be generated based on a quotation requested by a budget holder
- orders should be pre-numbered so that the company can control their issue. A copy will be sent to the accounts department and another copy to the goods inward department to tell them to expect a delivery
- the purchase order will be sent to a supplier who has previously been approved by the company. This approval means the supplier is considered reliable and able to deliver goods or services of the right quality, on time and at the agreed price
- when the goods are received they will be checked for quality and quantity by the goods inwards or inventory control staff and checked against the order. Details of the items received will be entered into the inventory records
- goods inwards staff will issue a pre-numbered goods received note and send a copy to the accounts department
- when the invoice from the supplier arrives the accounts department will match the details to their copy of the purchase order and the goods received note. This will ensure that the goods were ordered properly and that the company has actually received them
- once checked the invoice can be entered into the purchase day book or journal and from there to the nominal or general ledger and the purchase ledger
- a monthly statement from the supplier will be reconciled to the balance on the purchase ledger account to ensure all invoices, credit notes and payments have been properly recorded. This 'third party' confirmation is an excellent check for this

On receipt of the supplier statement or once the purchase invoice has been approved for payment and falls due, it will be paid.

In addition to the internal controls detailed above, the principle of segregation of duties applies in this system. The individuals who carry out each stage of the process should all be different so that no one individual can be involved with the whole transaction. This reduces the risk of errors or fraud on the part of the member of staff. A different person should ideally do each of the following:

- order goods
- deal with the movement of goods
- process invoices
- pay the invoices

purchases and cash payments system requirements

To re-cap – there are five main sections of the purchase system:

- placing the order
- receiving the goods
- receiving the invoice from the supplier
- recording the transaction in the accounts
- paying the invoice

The requirements for purchases can be identified for each stage of the purchases system as follows:

ordering

- all orders for goods and services are properly authorised
- orders are made only from approved suppliers

receipt of goods

- all goods and services received are for the purposes of the business and not for private use
- only goods and services that have been ordered are accepted
- goods ordered are received in a satisfactory condition
- unsatisfactory goods are returned to suppliers
- all receipts of goods and services are accurately recorded
- receipt of goods or services is evidenced

receipt of invoice

- liabilities are recognised for all goods and services received
- all invoices received are authorised
- any credits due to the business for faulty goods and services have been claimed
- liabilities can not be recorded for goods or services which have not been received or approved

accounting for purchases

- all expenditure is correctly recorded in the books and records of the business
- all credit notes are properly recorded in the books and records of the business
- all entries in the purchase ledger are to the correct suppliers' accounts
- all entries in the general ledger are to the correct account
- all purchases are recorded in the correct accounting period

payment

- all payments have been properly authorised
- all payments are for goods and services which have been received

purchases and cash payments system controls

Now that we have identified requirements of the purchases system, we can examine the controls information and procedures that the system should have in place to ensure that these requirements are achieved and also to minimise the risk of fraud and error.

Throughout the whole purchase process there should be formal written procedures for ordering, receiving and paying for goods and services.

Another key control within the system is segregation of duties – there should ideally be separate staff responsible for raising orders, receiving goods, and approving and paying invoices.

ordering

organisational controls
- ordering is only allowed from approved suppliers, accessed and set up only by specified individuals within the organisation

physical controls
- blank order forms are kept secure

authorisation
- there are recognised authority levels for orders above defined limits
- where purchase orders are computer-generated, only authorised individuals, using secure logins, are able to do so

arithmetic and accounting checks
- standard pre-numbered order forms are always used, stating quantity, price, delivery details
- regular review of orders placed but not received

receipt of goods

physical controls
- quantity and condition of goods received are properly checked
- pre-numbered goods received notes (GRNs) are always used stating quantity, description, date received, condition

authorisation
- GRNs are signed off for all goods received
- GRNs are matched to the order, which has been authorised

receipt of invoice and accounting

organisational controls	– stated authority levels should exist for approving invoices
authorisation	– all invoices are approved for payment
arithmetic and accounting checks	– invoices are matched with orders and GRNs
	– prices on invoices are agreed to standard supplier price lists and order forms
	– arithmetic accuracy of invoices is checked and evidenced
	– regular reconciliations of suppliers' statements with purchase ledger balances for accurate supplier account information
	– controls exist for processing purchase invoices (eg batch totals)
	– regular reconciliations of purchase ledger control account with purchase ledger balances and reconciling items investigated and cleared
	– period end checks are performed to ensure goods received but not invoiced are accounted for in the correct period

payment

physical controls	– cheque books are securely located
	– cancelled cheques are retained
authorisation	– recognised list of authorised cheque signatories or BACS approvals
	– a minimum of two cheque signatories for all payments or approvals for BACS payment
arithmetic and accounting checks	– regular bank reconciliation performed comparing cash book to bank statements and reconciling items investigated and cleared

Note: The bank reconciliation between the cash book and bank statements is an excellent way to ensure the cash book is complete and accurate, as the comparison is with a third party, ie the bank

potential errors if purchase system controls are not in place

If the client's system of internal control is weak and the internal controls are not working this increases the risk of some or all of the following:

- purchasing goods and services the company does not need
- failing to buy goods and services of the appropriate quality and at the lowest cost
- buying from unauthorised suppliers
- loss of discounts or bulk buying opportunities
- orders being placed by staff who are not authorised to do so
- orders being duplicated
- goods received not being checked for quality and quantity or accepted when not ordered
- fraud through the processing of false invoices or fraudulent payments
- invoices not being checked for receipt of order before being paid
- invoices being paid twice or not being paid at all, which may result in loss of supplier confidence
- poor cash flow if invoices are paid without taking advantage of credit terms and discounts
- incorrect inventory records
- incorrect costing records
- purchases and trade payables not being recorded accurately in the financial records
- incorrect period end procedures

THE REVENUE AND CASH RECEIPTS SYSTEM

system elements

The diagram on the next page shows the elements of a basic credit revenue system.

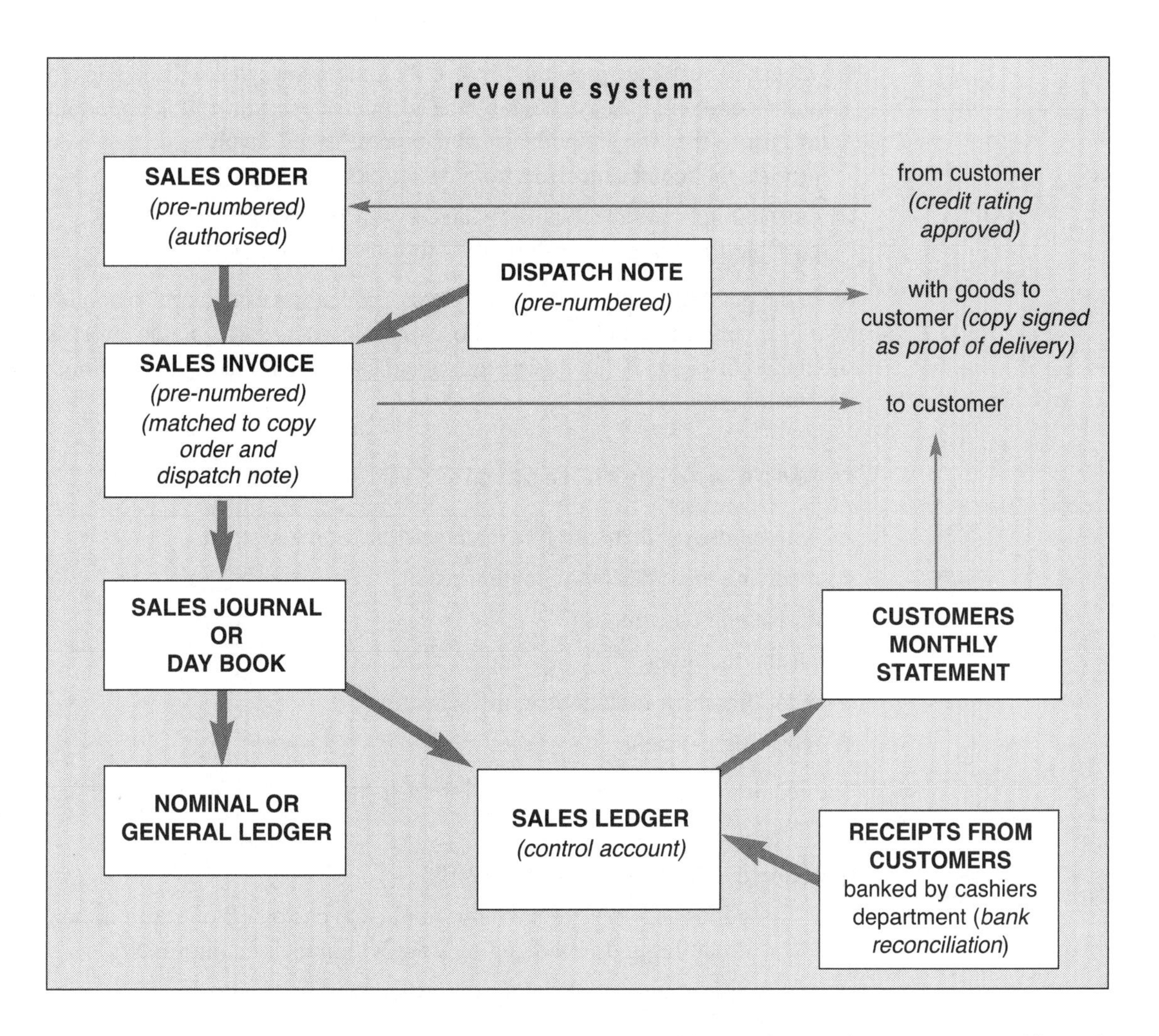

Within this system there are several internal controls. The system will work broadly like this:

- the sales orders will be taken by a sales department who will check the credit-worthiness of the customer
- goods will be despatched to the customer with a delivery note by the staff who deal with inventories and goods outwards. A copy of the delivery note will be signed by the customer and retained by the company as proof that the goods were delivered
- the sales invoice and the customer statement will be raised by the accounts department
- the accounts department will post the sales invoice to the sales day book or to a journal. From there they will post it to the sales ledger and the nominal or general ledger

- when the customer pays the invoice the money received will be banked and recorded in the cash book by the accounts department. It is important to ensure that the individuals who process sales invoices do not also process the monies received from customers
- outstanding trade receivables balances will be reviewed to identify any possible irrecoverable or doubtful debts and to chase slow payers

As in the purchases system the principle of segregation of duties also applies to this system. The individuals who carry out each stage of the process should be different so that no one individual can be involved with the whole transaction.

revenue and cash receipts system requirements

As with purchases there are five main sections of the system:

- receiving the order (and granting credit)
- despatching the goods
- raising the invoice
- recording the transactions in the accounts
- receiving payment

The requirements can be identified for each stage of the revenue system as follows:

receiving the order (and granting credit)

- goods and services are only supplied to customers on credit if their credit rating is good and they are within their credit limits
- orders are recorded correctly when they are received

despatching the goods

- goods are only despatched on the basis of approved orders
- all despatches of goods and services are accurately recorded
- all returns from customers are recorded and the reasons for rejection are investigated

invoicing

- all invoices raised relate to goods and services supplied by the business
- all despatches of goods or provision of services are invoiced at the correct price and on authorised terms
- credit notes are authorised and only issued for a valid reason

accounting for revenue

- all revenue is properly recorded in the books and records of the organisation
- all credit notes issued are properly recorded in the books and records of the organisation
- all entries in the sales ledger are to the correct customer accounts
- all entries in the general ledger are to the correct account
- all revenue has been recorded in the correct accounting period
- procedures exist for identifying irrecoverable debts

receiving payment (receipts)

- all receipts from customers have been properly recorded
- all payments received are for goods and services which have been supplied

revenue and cash receipts system controls

Now that we have identified the requirements of the revenue system, we can examine the controls information and procedures that the system should have in place to ensure that these requirements are achieved and also to minimise the risk of fraud and error.

In businesses where revenue involves a significant number of cash transactions, there is an increased risk of fraud and senior management hav[illegible] to be very aware of this. For this reason, cash sales will be [illegible] separately at the end of this section.

Throughout the revenue process there sho[illegible] for receiving orders, granting [illegible] payment for goods and [illegible]

There should a[illegible] staff responsible [illegible] receiving paymen[illegible]

receiving orders an[illegible]

organisational [illegible]

physical controls	– blank sales order forms are kept secure
authorisation	– there are recognised authority levels for changes in customer data (eg increasing discount allowed) – all increases to customer credit limits are authorised
arithmetic and accounting checks	– pre-numbered sales order forms are always used stating quantity, price, description, delivery details, discounts – prices quoted to customers are checked to standard price list and appropriate discounts applied

despatching goods

organisational controls	– delivery notes are matched with orders and invoices
physical controls	– the quantity and condition of goods supplied are properly checked – pre-numbered delivery notes should always be used – proof of delivery is obtained for all goods despatched (signed delivery notes) – returns from customers are recorded (pre-numbered goods returned notes issued by the buyer) and reasons investigated

invoicing and accounting for revenue

organisational controls	– invoices and credit notes are pre-numbered and sequentially issued, and spoilt invoices are not destroyed
authorisation	– all credit notes are authorised – all non-standard discounts are approved
arithmetic and accounting checks	– invoices are matched with orders and delivery notes – prices on invoices are agreed to standard price lists or appropriate costing information and discount information – VAT rates are verified on the invoice – credit notes are matched with goods returned notes and the reason recorded

- controls are in place for processing invoices (eg batch totals)
- invoices and credit notes entered into the accounting records promptly
- invoices and credit notes are posted to the correct customer account
- regular up-to-date statements are sent to customers
- regular reconciliation of the sales ledger control account with sales ledger balances
- period end checks are performed to ensure goods that have been despatched but not invoiced are accounted for in the correct period

receiving payment (receipts)

physical controls

- all money received from customers is initially recorded by two people
- all money received is banked intact on the same day using paying in slips

arithmetic and accounting checks

- regular bank reconciliations are performed comparing the cash book and bank statement and investigating differences using paying in slips, BACS records etc
- all cash received is posted to the correct customer account

potential errors if revenue and cash receipts system controls are not in place

If the internal control requirements are not working then there is an increased risk of the following:

- selling to non creditworthy customers
- failure to record customer orders and therefore supplying incorrect or incomplete orders or not supplying at all and losing a sales opportunity
- goods or services being supplied without being invoiced
- duplication of sales invoices
- sales invoices not being checked before despatch, and issued with incorrect figures
- incorrect VAT calculations

- goods and services sold at the wrong price
- credit notes being issued for something other than goods returned, for example fraudulently writing off debts
- incorrect inventory records, despatches not being recorded correctly or theft of inventory not being detected
- poor credit control resulting in weak cash management
- sales and trade receivables not being recorded accurately and correctly in the financial records
- theft of money received from customers
- incorrect cut-off procedures

cash sales system

There are certain types of business where a significant volume of revenue is received in cash. Examples include supermarkets, bars, restaurants, taxi firms and hairdressers. You will be able to think of others.

When designing procedures for these types of organisations, the directors or senior management have to consider the increased likelihood of fraud. Inadequate controls in the client system over the collection and recording of cash receipts could lead to misappropriation of cash.

Consequently there are additional controls that need to be in place to ensure the accuracy of the recording of cash sales and the certainty that all of them have been recorded.

Additional controls for cash sales include:

- all cash sales to be recorded using a till (credit card sales would also be recorded here under a separate category)
- authorised staff perform a daily cash count at the end of the day and ensure the correct amount is entered onto daily takings sheet
- daily takings sheet matching the cash sales per the till receipt to the cash banked to be completed
- differences between cash sales per the till and cash to be banked to be investigated
- if cash is held overnight, it is kept in a secure locked location, eg a safe
- cash receipts to be bank intact daily
- if any items, such as wages, small bills or petty cash items paid are out of cash, they are to be supported with documentation (receipts, timesheet) and a reconciliation of till cash banked to be completed

THE PAYROLL SYSTEM

The payroll system contains details of the organisation's staff and their wages and salary payments. The organisation's requirements when operating the payroll system are to ensure that it pays the correct rate of pay for the actual amount of work done.

The principal differences between wages and salaries are:

- wages tend to be paid weekly and salaries monthly
- wages can vary from week to week, whereas salaries are generally a set payment, and only vary if commission or bonus payments are included

It is becoming increasingly rare for wages to be paid in cash; for security reasons most staff are paid directly into their bank account by BACS. If payments are still made in cash there are a number of issues that are raised which we will look at later in this section.

Key points that relate to both wages and salaries are:

- all employees must have a contract or written terms of employment
- rates of pay must be agreed
- all deductions from gross pay must be statutory (eg PAYE and NI) or authorised by the employee (eg pension contributions)
- there are defined rules for calculating tax and national insurance contributions, whatever method is used for paying staff
- staff must be paid regularly and on time
- payroll must comply with taxation rules eg, real time information for HMRC

Businesses may have a mixture of staff paid a weekly wage and staff paid a monthly salary. In this case they may operate two payrolls. If this is the case, directors must ensure information requirements are met and controls are in place for each payroll to ensure that both are operated correctly.

confidentiality

In Chapter 3 we explained how accounts staff must treat all the information they have access to on a day-to-day basis as confidential. This is particularly important when dealing with payroll. Matters such as rates of pay and individual's salaries can be a very sensitive area and one that can be of particular interest to other employees!

The payroll system contains much personal information about employees including:

- the hourly rate of pay or annual salary
- additional benefits
- home address
- bank details
- date of birth
- national insurance number

It is the duty of the organisation under the Data Protection Act to ensure that all this information remains confidential.

system elements

The diagram below shows the components of a basic payroll system, whether for wages or salaries. (*Internal controls* are shown in italics.)

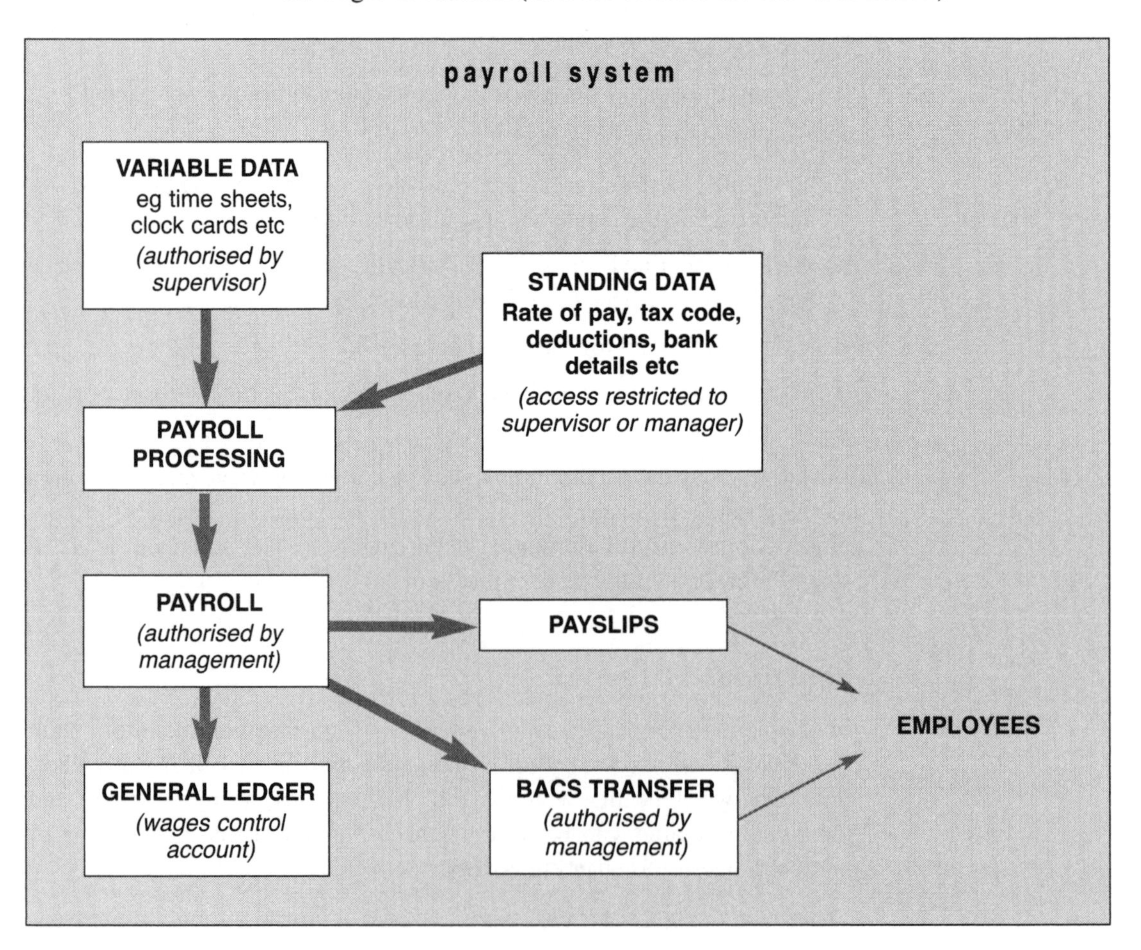

In contrast to the purchases and revenue systems we have looked at, there is a limited segregation of duties within a payroll system as, normally, the payroll is prepared by staff in one department who carry out the entire process.

The actual payment of wages or salaries is made by the accounts department but it is the payroll staff who tell them how much to pay to whom.

The key controls in the payroll system are authorisation and management review.

The system works broadly like this:

- variable data such as overtime or hours worked for casual workers is approved by a manager based on some form of time recording. This could be a clock card or a time sheet. The hours to be paid should be validated and authorised before being input to the payroll system
- salaried staff who are not paid overtime are paid a regular amount each month. However any additional payments such as bonuses or commission should also be authorised
- the computer will contain a master file which contains fixed data about each employee. Such data includes:
  - staff number
  - rate of pay (hourly, weekly, monthly)
  - tax code
  - National Insurance (NI) number
  - deductions such as pension contributions, subscriptions, student loans, court orders etc
  - bank details – sort code and account number
- the payroll software applies the variable data to the standing data and calculates:
  - gross pay
  - deductions (PAYE, NIC, others as notified)
  - net pay
  - gross taxable pay to date
  - tax paid to date
- the software also prepares a payments list; in most cases employees are paid by automatic bank transfers using the Banks Automated Credit System (BACS)
- payslips are prepared to be sent to each employee
- the payroll should be approved by management
- the BACS payment list must be signed ideally by two authorised signatories
- payment is made by direct transfer originated by the accounts department

payroll system requirements

The main stages of the payroll system are as follows:

- hours are input into the system as required and amendments to staff details are made when necessary
- gross pay, deductions and net pay are calculated and payslips produced
- transactions are recorded in the accounts
- payments are made to staff and HM Revenue & Customs

The requirements for the system can be identified for each stage of the system as follows:

inputting hours and amending staff details

- all amendments to staff details are properly authorised
- hours worked are approved at an appropriate level
- staff are only paid for hours worked
- only staff who work for the company are included on the payroll
- details of leavers and joiners are authorised and promptly entered onto the payroll system
- staff details remain confidential at all times

calculating payroll and deductions

- payroll is calculated based on approved rates and hours worked
- statutory deductions for PAYE and NI are correctly calculated
- voluntary deductions (eg pension contributions or share save schemes) are correctly calculated

accounting for payroll and payments to staff and HM Revenue & Customs

- net pay is accurately calculated and paid to the correct employee
- payroll figures are correctly recorded in the books and records of the business, including pension contributions, share save schemes etc
- all payments for PAYE and NI are paid on the due date
- wages and salaries are paid on the right date

payroll system controls

Now that we have identified the requirements of the payroll system, we can examine the controls information and procedures that the system should have in place to ensure that these information requirements are achieved and the risk of fraud and error minimised.

Throughout the whole payroll process there should be formal written procedures for recording and inputting hours worked, amending staff details, and paying wages and salaries.

There should also be segregation of duties between staff responsible for approving hours worked, making changes to staff details and inputting and calculating payments. Where wages are paid in cash, one person should be responsible for counting the cash and another more senior person should check the amounts paid.

inputting hours and amending staff details

organisational controls

- a written record such as a contract of employment, is kept for each employee containing details of rates of pay and contracted hours; any changes should require appropriate authorisation
- formal procedures are followed for starters and leavers
- timesheets and clock cards are approved before hours are entered onto the payroll system

physical controls

- access to the payroll office is restricted to authorised personnel only
- access to the payroll and staff records is restricted to authorised personnel only

authorisation

- all changes to rates of pay, bonus payments and commission earned should be authorised
- written approval from employees should be obtained for all voluntary deductions from wages or salaries

arithmetic and accounting controls

- all timesheets to be added up to ensure accuracy

calculating payroll and deductions

organisational controls	– up-to-date versions of payroll software should be installed, using the latest tax and national insurance rates – staff are fully trained on PAYE and NI issues – changes to staff tax codes are promptly and accurately entered on the payroll system
authorisation	– payroll schedules are approved before payment
arithmetic and accounting checks	– wages and salaries control account is regularly reconciled – commission and bonuses are reconciled to source documentation (eg sales records) – piecework payments (ie payments based on the number of items produced) are regularly reviewed against levels of work completed – unusual changes in payments to individuals from month to month are identified

accounting for payroll and payments to staff and HM Revenue & Customs

organisational controls	– a timetable for payment of wages and salaries is maintained and adhered to
physical controls	– staff who count wages in cash are not the same as those who prepare the payroll – at least two staff handle cash for wages – cash for payment of wages is stored securely at all times – payslips are handed to staff members personally or are sent to their home address in sealed envelopes
authorisation	– pay packets can only be signed for by the individual staff member – BACS payment schedules are authorised by an appropriate person before processing

arithmetic and accounting checks	– the wages control account is regularly reconciled – a comparison is made between wages paid and budgeted figures for wages by department – a regular check is made of deductions by accounts staff to ensure consistency with previous periods' deductions – reconciliations are regularly performed between the total net pay figure and payment shown on the bank statement – a regular review of National Insurance and PAYE accounts to ensure no outstanding balances remain after payment to HM Revenue & Customs

potential errors if payroll system controls are not in place

The risks to the business if the controls are not working are:

- paying for work which has not been carried out
- incorrect gross pay calculation
- paying people who are not employees, ie those who have left the business
- failure to pay new employees
- failure to pay wages and salaries on the correct date
- incorrect calculation of net pay
- failing to deduct correct amounts of tax and National Insurance
- failure to pay amounts due to HMRC on time
- paying 'ghost' workers ie fictitious employees fraudulently included on payroll
- amounts for wages and salaries incorrectly recorded in financial and costing records

COSTING SYSTEM

system components

The diagram below shows the elements of a basic costing system. (*Internal controls are shown in italics.*)

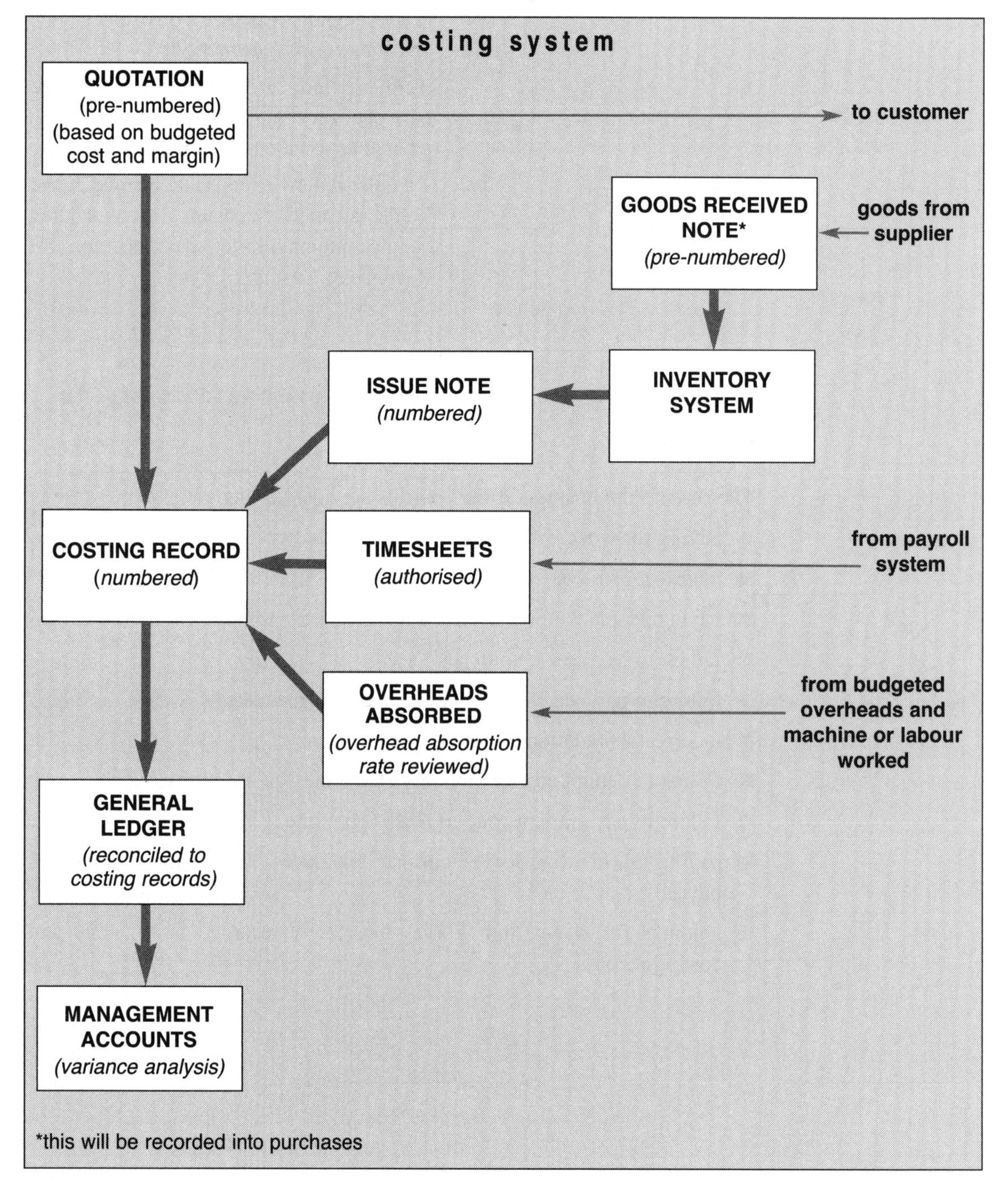

Within this system there are a number of internal controls. The system works broadly like this:

- the business will use a method of costing, such as job, process or batch costing
- it will gather information about how much each product costs to make, including direct materials, direct labour and direct expenses
- direct material costs will come from sources such as a supplier's price list or the value of inventory currently held
- direct labour costs will be estimated using current wages rates and an estimate of how long the work will take
- direct expenses, such as royalties, will be based on current contractual information
- indirect production overheads will be included in the cost of a product using a calculated Overhead Absorption Rate (OAR), based on budgeted overheads
- an allowance will be made for non-production overheads
- the product will be priced using an authorised margin or mark up policy or for the product line
- actual materials, labour and overhead costs will be collected and the product or job will be recorded as finished goods in inventory in the general ledger
- a comparison will be made between the standard and actual cost for a product or job to produce a variance analysis, as part of the Management Accounts production process
- the variances will be investigated by management to determine why they occurred and whether the business needs to review its costing for future products or jobs or if the costing system is working accurately
- materials price and usage and labour rate and efficiency variances may be produced to enable further analysis of why variances have occurred
- overhead absorption rates will be investigated to ensure they accurately reflect the overheads which need to be recovered
- when goods are sold, the Cost of Sales figure will be updated and the inventory value reduced accordingly

As mentioned in the previous systems, segregation of duties is important. Those who cost the product should not be able to charge material costs to a job and then investigate any arising variance.

costing system requirements

There are five main sections of the system:

- Costing of a product, job, batch or process
- Pricing a product, job, batch or process
- Inventory management
- Accounting for costing the product, job, batch or process
- Calculating and investigating the variances between budgeted (costed) product, job, batch or process and the actual costs

The requirements can be identified for each stage of the costing system as follows:

costing of a product, job, batch or process

- goods are costed to include all direct costs
- costing includes a relevant proportion of production overheads, usually through a budgeted overhead absorption rate (OAR)

pricing a product, job, batch or process

- all prices are determined using the costing information and an allowance for non-production overheads
- all prices include an element of profit, either by marking up total cost or adding on a margin

inventory management

- materials ordered for the job are compared to the order, to ensure they are necessary
- materials ordered for the job are inspected on delivery to ensure they are of appropriate quality and complete
- materials received are accurately booked into stores as inventory
- materials are stored securely
- all inventory is accurately booked out of stores
- physical inventory is periodically compared to the inventory records to ensure the accuracy of the stores booking in and out process

accounting for costing the product, job, batch or process

- inventory is charged to the correct product, job, batch or process
- direct labour costs are collected and charged to the product, job, batch or process via timesheets or an electronic recording system
- direct expenses are collected and allocated to each job correctly
- OAR are accurately charged to the product, job, batch or process based on machine or labour hours
- overheads are accurately recorded in the general ledger
- all costs collected are accurately recorded in the general ledger as inventory, until sold
- all jobs are recorded accurately in 'cost of sales' and removed from inventory when sold

calculating and investigating the variances between budgeted and actual costs

- all variances between actual and budgeted costs are calculated and reasons investigated
- if standard costing is used, material usage and price variances are accurately calculated and reasons investigated
- if standard costing is used, labour rate and efficiency variances are accurately calculated and reasons investigated
- actual overhead is compared to absorbed overhead and differences investigated

costing system controls

Now that we have looked at the requirements of a costing system, we can examine the controls, information and procedures that the system should have in place to ensure these requirements are achieved and also to minimise the risk of fraud and error.

Throughout the costing system and inventory management there should be formal written procedures for costing a product, pricing a product, inventory management, charging the actual costs of production to the product, job or batch and calculating and investigating variances between budgeted and actual costs.

There should be segregation of duties within the system with different staff responsible for costing products, controlling inventory and investigating variances.

costing of a product, job or batch

organisational control	– there are recognised procedures for costing a new product or providing a quotation for a customer
personnel	– competent, trained staff are used for costing products
authorisation	– there are recognised authority levels for approval of costing for products or jobs
	– all changes to the build up (or bill of materials) of a product cost are authorised, including updating standard material or labour costs for standard costing systems
arithmetic and accounting checks	– pre-numbered quotations are always used
	– each product or job has its own unique reference number, linked to its costing record
	– all costings are checked for arithmetical accuracy
	– overhead absorption rates are calculated based on budgeted overheads accurately

pricing a product, job or batch

organisational controls	– the pricing policy is always adhered to
	– there are recognised levels of authority for discounts or amendments to pricing
	– quotations are pre-numbered and sequentially issued
arithmetic and accounting checks	– margin or mark-up are checked for arithmetical accuracy

inventory management

organisational controls	– there are procedures for the receipt and issue of inventory into and out of stores
physical controls	– inventory is stored in a secure location, accessed only by the Stores staff
	– inventory is housed appropriately, to keep it in good condition
	– inventory received is matched to an order

- goods received notes are issued with each delivery
- goods received notes are issued with each delivery
- the quality and condition of goods supplier are properly checked
- returns to suppliers are recorded (pre-numbered goods returned notes) and reasons investigated

arithmetic and accounting checks

- goods issued to production or each job are recorded using a unique pre-numbered issues note
- periodical inventory counts are performed matching physical items to the records and vice versa to confirm the existence of inventory and the accuracy of the records
- regular reconciliation of the inventory records to the general ledger

accounting for costing the product, job or batch

organisational controls

- there are clear procedures for recording costs against jobs or products

arithmetic and accounting checks

- direct materials costs are charged to each job, on the basis of FIFO or AVCO methods of valuing issues, via the unique product or job code, using a unique pre-numbered sequential issue note
- direct labour costs are always charged to the job or product using information from timesheets and the unique job number
- OAR are charged to the job or product based on actual machine hours or labour hours for the job, using the unique job number
- regular review of under or over absorbed overheads and whether the OAR needs to be updated

	– review of production overheads recorded in the general ledger for accuracy
	– direct material, labour and expenses costs are promptly posted to product production or the job
	– automatic updating from the costing system to the general ledger
	– regular reconciliation of costing system to general ledger

calculating and investigating the variances between budgeted and actual costs

organisational controls	– there are recognised procedures for investigating variances
arithmetic and accounting checks	– all variances are calculated for each period for each job or product
	– all material price and usage variances are calculated each period within a standard costing system and reasons investigated
	– all labour rate and usage variances are calculated each period within a standard costing system and reasons investigated
	– under or over absorbed overheads are posted to the profit and loss account at the end of the period and reasons for them investigated
	– the gross profit margin is reviewed periodically to ensure it is at expected levels
management	– all significant variances are investigated by appropriately senior, qualified staff

potential errors if the costing system controls are not in place

If the internal controls are not working, then there is an increased risk of the following:

- costing will not include all direct costs, so pricing will be too low, lowering profitability of the business
- overhead costs will not be included, so pricing will be too low
- pricing will not include a suitable profit element
- unnecessary items may be received which have not been ordered
- materials may be received which are of unsatisfactory quality or quantity
- inventory records could be inaccurate, causing production delays
- inventory could be booked against the wrong job
- inventory could be stolen
- inventory could be damaged
- actual material and labour costs of a job could be inaccurate, leading to inaccurate variance analysis
- costing and pricing of future jobs could be inaccurate if based on inaccurate previous actual information
- excessive wastage could continue to occur
- material prices used to costs products could be too low
- inefficient working practices of employees could be unchallenged
- labour rated used to cost products could be too low
- overhead absorption rates could be out of date, so overheads could be consistently under or over recovered
- the value of inventory, which will use OARs as part of the valuation, could be under or overstated in the financial statements, under or overstating profit for the year
- cost of sales and the value of inventory not being recorded accurately and correctly in the financial records

CAPITAL EXPENDITURE SYSTEM

system elements

When a business is considering purchasing a capital item, it is investing in its future, so the capital expenditure process is slightly different, as shown in the diagram on the next page. (Note that internal controls are shown in italics.)

As you can see, the capital expenditure system differs from the purchases system in two main areas – initial approval and the asset register, used for recording and the ongoing control of the asset. Therefore, we will just focus on these two different areas.

approval

The capital expenditure approval system is different, as the items being bought could be for several thousands of pounds.

- As part of the budgeting process, in order to ensure the business really needs the item being purchased, management will look at how they plan to meet the future needs of the business in terms of plant, equipment, machinery, buildings and vehicles for the short, medium and longer term. Initially they will usually consider up to five years of potential investment, with a detailed capital expenditure budget for the first year.
- If the business is a limited company, the capital expenditure budget will normally be approved by the Board of Directors, prior to the start of the year.
- Capital items are authorised by being included in the capital expenditure budget. They are likely to be purchased either from an approved supplier or by a tendering process, with a minimum of three suppliers being considered, to ensure the price and service will be as the business requires. Once a supplier is agreed on, a purchase order will be raised as in the purchases system.

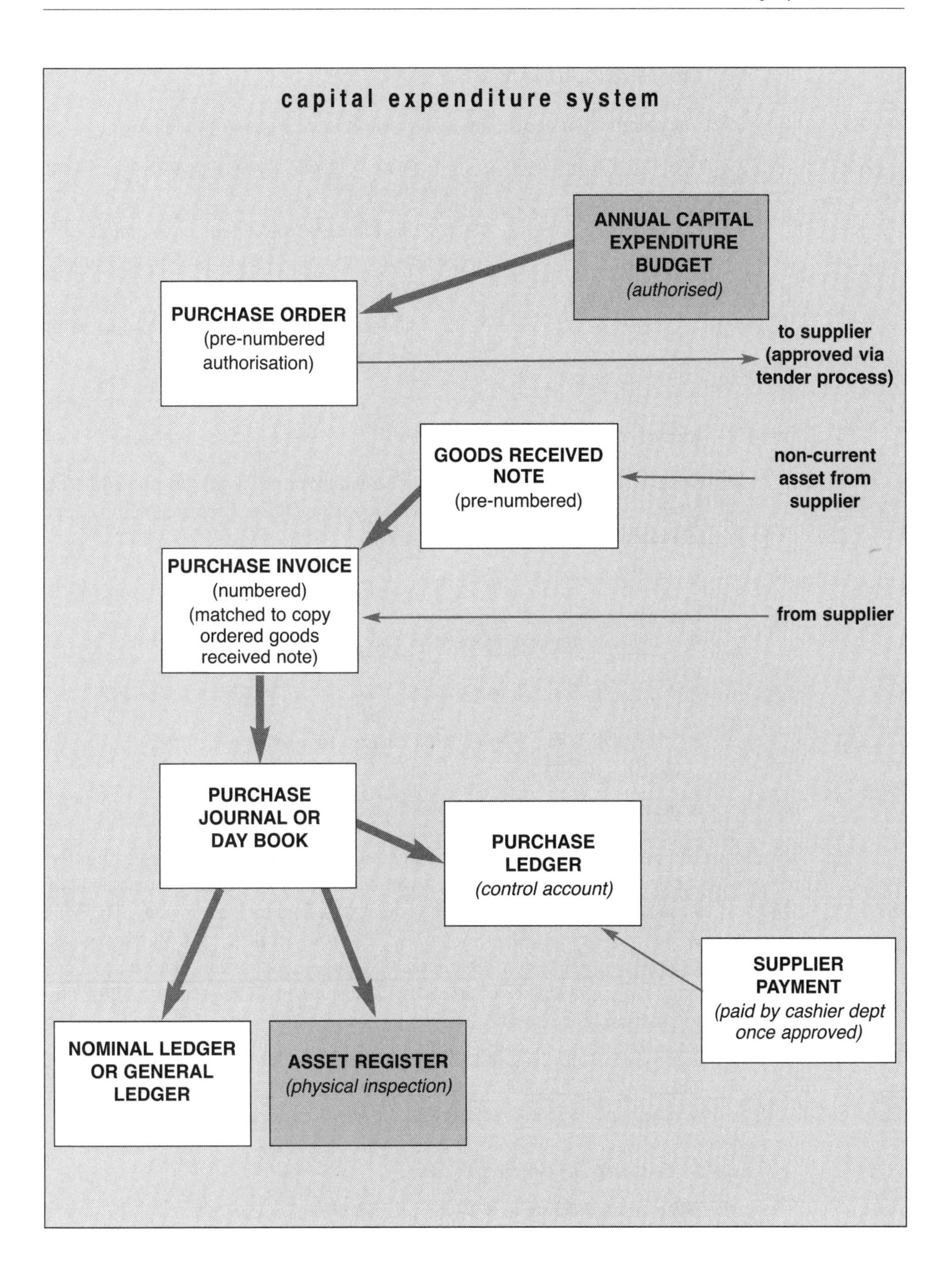
capital expenditure system
ANNUAL CAPITAL EXPENDITURE BUDGET
(authorised)
PURCHASE ORDER
(pre-numbered authorisation)
to supplier (approved via tender process)
GOODS RECEIVED NOTE
(pre-numbered)
non-current asset from supplier
PURCHASE INVOICE
(numbered)
(matched to copy ordered goods received note)
from supplier
PURCHASE JOURNAL OR DAY BOOK
PURCHASE LEDGER
(control account)
SUPPLIER PAYMENT
(paid by cashier dept once approved)
NOMINAL LEDGER OR GENERAL LEDGER
ASSET REGISTER
(physical inspection)

approval controls

The controls within the approval part of the system are listed below:

organisational controls – ordering is by a tendering process, using approved suppliers

authorisation – the Board approve the capital expenditure budget for the year, as part of a 5 year or longer plan

– the purchase order is approved in line with capital expenditure authorisation budget

asset register

Once a capital item has been received and invoiced, it will be entered in the general ledger as a non-current asset. A detailed asset register will be kept recording the following:

- purchase date
- supplier
- unique reference number (item may be barcoded – see below)
- cost
- useful life
- depreciation rate, depreciation charged to date
- location/department
- responsible manager/employee

The asset register forms the main record for non-current assets for the business. As it is so detailed, it can be used for controlling movements of these assets and for ensuring they are all still held by the company. This will be done by periodically comparing all the physical items with the register and following up any differences. In a large organisation, where there are many types and classes of assets, the assets might be barcoded, to allow this comparison process to be as fast and efficient as possible.

When assets are disposed of, there should be an authorisation process in place, so only authorised people are able to make the sale. You would not want anyone to be able to sell the company's factory!

asset register controls

The controls relating to the asset register are set out below:

authorisation – disposal of assets and removal from the register will be approved by authorised people

physical	– assets are barcoded and secured where possible
	– ownership documents are securely stored
arithmetic and accounting	– regular reconciliation of the asset register to physical assets held and differences investigated
	– reconciliation of asset register to general or nominal ledger on a regular basis eg monthly for cost, depreciation and carrying value

potential errors if capital expenditure system controls are not in place

If the internal controls in the capital expenditure system are not in place, including those in the purchases system discussed above, this increases the risk of some or all of the following:

- purchasing capital items that the company does not need
- failing to buy capital items of the appropriate quality and at the lowest cost
- buying from unauthorised suppliers
- loss of discount opportunities
- orders being placed by staff who are not authorised to do so
- capital items being paid for when they are not working
- incorrect general ledger
- capital items being misplaced or removed from the company
- inaccurate depreciation calculations
- disposals being made without appropriate authorisation and at a below market value
- the financial statements not reflecting the correct non-current asset information, depreciation expense and disposal information

THE VALUE OF AN INTEGRATED SYSTEM

integration and authorisation

A well organised system should ideally be an integrated computerised system on a network using proprietory software such as Sage and Microsoft Office. All the accounting systems should integrate (link) together, so the general ledger is up to date and accurate. Information should only need to be entered manually once, reducing the risk of errors or fraud.

As the whole system is linked, the company should consider who should be able to see what. As previously stated, segregation is critical to minimising the risk of fraud, so people should only be given access to those parts of the system which they need to do their job effectively. To maintain this, accounting staff will have their own passwords authorising which areas of the system they can access. For example, the Payroll Clerk should be able to access the payroll system but not the general ledger or cashbook. These passwords should be kept confidential and be of a secure nature – often passwords now must contain letters, numbers, lower and upper case items and unusual characters. Wag3s!pa4 would be a strong password, as long as it is not written on a post-it next to the Payroll Clerk's desk!

reporting and monitoring using an integrated system

Where a system is integrated, data can be extracted very easily and in a prompt and user-friendly manner. This allows the company to monitor its activities well and to produce reports as and when necessary. For example, payroll could be analysed by department or by job, to see where efficiencies might be made. If the company was using job costing, reports on jobs where the margin earned is below set limits could be produced to investigate what action needs to be taken to ensure the profitability of future jobs. Also the company can produce management accounts promptly and take corrective or preventative action to improve future performance.

An integrated system can also assist in meeting the needs of other stakeholders. For example, customers want invoicing to be prompt and accurate, with accurate monthly statements, clearly showing payments they have made and an integrated revenue system will give this. Similarly, suppliers require accurate information, so all invoices will be correctly recorded and the ledger accurately reflects their transactions with the business.

HOW EFFECTIVE SYSTEMS CAN SUPPORT ETHICAL PRACTICE AND SUSTAINABILITY

ethical considerations

A system with strong internal controls can not only be effective in recording and controlling the transactions of the company, it can also support ethical values. By having controls in place, it can ensure ethical principles are met on a daily basis.

The relevant ethical principles as explained on pages 46-49 are:

- Objectivity
- Integrity
- Professional Behaviour
- Professional Competence and Due Care
- Confidentiality

The following table gives examples of some different systems, the controls within them and how they support ethical principles (in italics):

payroll	– only payroll staff can access staff data (*confidentiality*)
	– wages can only be collected by the person being paid and are signed for (*professional competence and due care*)
revenue	– credit limits are set using a credit control policy (*objectivity*)
	– overdue debts are chased according to a detailed credit control policy for all customers (*objectivity*)
	– discounts are applied according to company policy and communicated to customers (*integrity*)
	– credit control staff are trained to deal with late payers in an appropriate manner and following the credit control policy (*professional behaviour*)
purchases	– the tendering process is clear and specified (*professional behaviour, objectivity*)
	– when goods are received they are compared to the order and the physical condition of them is checked (*professional competence and due care*)
	– supplier payments are made in line with supplier terms (*integrity*)

sustainable considerations

Just as an effective system can support ethical practice, it can also support sustainability. For example, having a long-term pricing policy with a customer for a set period of time will encourage a long-term relationship, supporting economic growth for both your company and the customer. If a company invests in qualifications for Account Receivable staff, who can then undertake efficient and effective Credit Control, they will improve the future earnings and social well being of that individual. Finally a tendering policy for capital equipment could only consider suppliers who undertaken sustainable production practices, to support these goals.

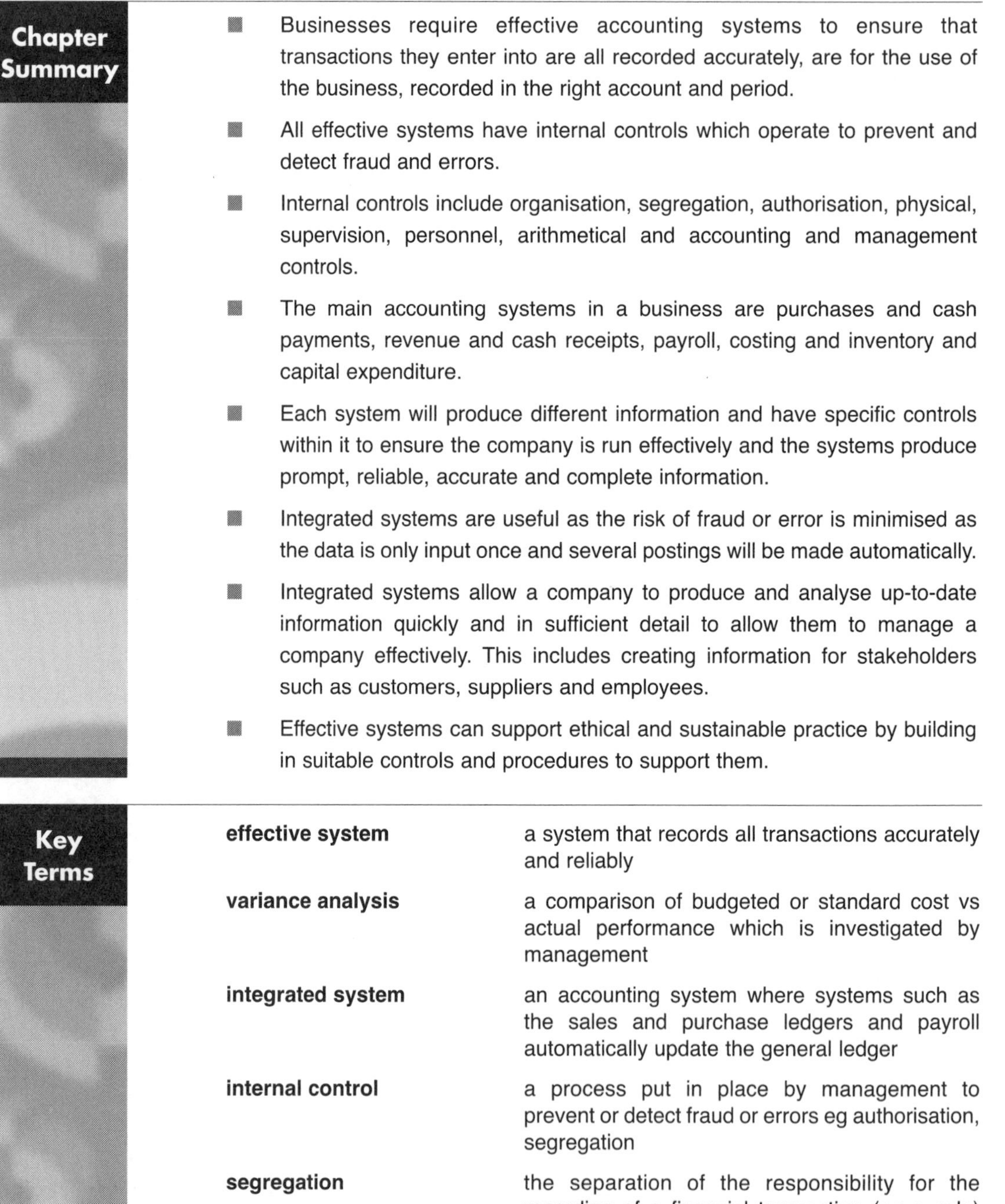

Chapter Summary

- Businesses require effective accounting systems to ensure that transactions they enter into are all recorded accurately, are for the use of the business, recorded in the right account and period.
- All effective systems have internal controls which operate to prevent and detect fraud and errors.
- Internal controls include organisation, segregation, authorisation, physical, supervision, personnel, arithmetical and accounting and management controls.
- The main accounting systems in a business are purchases and cash payments, revenue and cash receipts, payroll, costing and inventory and capital expenditure.
- Each system will produce different information and have specific controls within it to ensure the company is run effectively and the systems produce prompt, reliable, accurate and complete information.
- Integrated systems are useful as the risk of fraud or error is minimised as the data is only input once and several postings will be made automatically.
- Integrated systems allow a company to produce and analyse up-to-date information quickly and in sufficient detail to allow them to manage a company effectively. This includes creating information for stakeholders such as customers, suppliers and employees.
- Effective systems can support ethical and sustainable practice by building in suitable controls and procedures to support them.

Key Terms

effective system — a system that records all transactions accurately and reliably

variance analysis — a comparison of budgeted or standard cost vs actual performance which is investigated by management

integrated system — an accounting system where systems such as the sales and purchase ledgers and payroll automatically update the general ledger

internal control — a process put in place by management to prevent or detect fraud or errors eg authorisation, segregation

segregation — the separation of the responsibility for the recording of a financial transaction (eg a sale) and the responsibility for the recording of its settlement (ie the customer paying)

physical control — the use of physical security to prevent fraud, such as a safe or locked cupboard or drawer

overhead absorption rate (OAR) — the rate used to charge overheads to cost units

5.1 You have been asked to set up a 10-character password for Design for Life Ltd's payroll system. Which **one** of the following is the most secure?

(a) 1march1976	
(b) Two*Nine-7	
(c) 0987654321	
(d) password16	

5.2 You are the Financial Controller of a chain of travel agents and are training a new Purchase Ledger Clerk on the reconciliation of the purchase ledger to the purchase ledger control account, a key internal control. The Purchase Ledger Clerk asks you 'By doing this does this mean that there will be no problems or errors on the purchase ledger?'

Explain whether the Purchase Ledger Clerk's comment is correct or not, giving examples to support your case.

5.3 You have been asked to specify a new sales system for Trampolines For Fun Limited. Give examples of the types of controls you would look to include in the system for :

- receiving the order and granting credit to customers
- despatching the goods
- raising the invoice
- recording the transaction in the accounts
- receiving payment

5.4 You are S. Poak, the Accountant for Pedal for Miles Limited, a company making bicycles, which employs 60 staff. The payroll bureau that currently manages payroll has become increasingly expensive, so you have been asked to investigate what the company would need to put in place to allow it to manage its own payroll system

Write an email setting out the main elements of a payroll system to S. Addle, your Managing Director.

5.5 Set out the key controls you would expect to use when making capital purchases and managing the asset register in a company.

5.6 What type of potential issues within a company does an effective costing system prevent?

6 Evaluation and review of an accounting system

this chapter covers...

In this chapter we look at the issues involved in evaluating and reviewing an accounting system.

The review will involve assessing the strengths of the accounting system:

- *seeing how the underlying procedures fulfil the needs of the organisation and its operation*
- *seeing how effective the internal control system is in terms of procedures*

The review will then assess the weaknesses of the accounting system, analysing:

- *weaknesses in the accounting system and company procedures*
- *the possibilities for error and fraud involving the loss of money, inventory and reputation*
- *ways in which sustainable development policies and ethical procedures are supported by the company's procedures*

We will look at how these weaknesses impact on the company, including:

- *cost, reliability and speed*
- *time, money and reputation*

Finally we will consider how a SWOT analysis can help us evaluate the internal controls in an accounting system

REVIEWING THE ACCOUNTING SYSTEM AND UNDERLYING PROCEDURES

As each organisation grows and changes different accounting systems and policies will be implemented or discarded. When a small business is set up, the accounting systems may be quite basic and only have limited controls. This is because the accounts are prepared by few people and a small number of people are involved in decision – making, so there is no need for systems to be complex.

As a business grows and employs more people, produces more products and sells more goods, the accounting systems it needs will be different. The business may have several members of accounts, not just one or two, so the systems in place and the information being generated will be significant in volume and is likely to be complex, with different departments requesting information. And so, to ensure the accounting system is 'fit for purpose' it will need to be regularly reviewed. As part of the synoptic assessment, you will be asked to review the adequacy of one or more of the accounting systems. This will be based on the organisation in the pre-release material, so you will have some prior knowledge of its structure. The review could cover the following areas:

- The accounting records and financial reporting information: are they sufficient and do they provide the necessary information the company and stakeholders need?
- The internal control systems: how efficient are they in terms of detecting errors and preventing fraud and do they support ethical standards and sustainable practices?
- Methods of working: do current practices support the business and its future? Are the computers systems in place to meet the information needs of the company? Are the procedures and processes fit for purpose?

To allow you to review a system thoroughly, you will need to assess the **strengths** of the existing system – in terms of its controls and procedures. You will then need to analysis the **weaknesses** of the system. To help you do this, you could produce a SWOT analysis of the procedures. We will look at one of these at the end of Chapter 7, as this will include potential **opportunities** and **threats** as well.

IDENTIFYING THE STRENGTHS OF THE SYSTEM

There are various areas of investigation which will indicate how effective the accounting system is in preventing errors and detecting and deterring fraud. Using the pre-release material given, you could:

- draw up an organisational chart of the accounting system showing the areas of responsibility and the various reporting lines
- draw up a plan of the system, noting who completes which activities and the controls over each step, similar to the system diagrams in the previous chapter
- identify the other operational areas of the organisation which the accounting system supports

You can consider areas which relate to a number of different aspects of internal control by asking a number of questions:

operating procedures, reliability and efficiency?

'Is there a Policies and Procedures (or similar) document?'

'Is the authorisation system for payments clear and workable?'

'Are there the necessary routine checking procedures in place?'

'Are there random checks made to ensure procedures are being followed correctly?'

'Are the records kept in an organised way?'

'Are passwords (both to computers and premises) kept secure and changed when necessary?'

'Are items such as the petty cash box and the company cheque books kept under lock and key and are the keys kept only by authorised staff?'

'Are the reporting lines within the organisation working efficiently?'

'Is the system cost-effective – does it use resources efficiently?'

'Does the system support sustainable practices, eg suppliers who have sustainable policies, sourcing goods locally?'

'Are there safeguards to ensure ethical behaviour, eg confidentiality guidelines?'

'Is the system completely reliable, eg if staff are away?'

So where the answer to the question is above is 'yes' then we can state the system is a strong effective system.

computer systems

The computer system should be integrated, so that all the ledgers automatically update the general ledger, using software such as Sage or Microsoft office. There should also be IT authorisation controls in place, so that users can only access the parts of the system they need to use in their job. This keeps the data protected and ultimately, reliable.

By having an integrated system, the business should be able to generate good quality information as and when it is needed. A good computerised system will support the business, so the reports it generates will provide relevant information in a format the managers need and understand. For example, a good system will allow the Financial Controller to produce an income statement, to meet financial reporting requirements as well as the information needed to run and manage the business, for example:

- revenue and costs by product line or location
- labour costs broken down by department, split into indirect and direct costs
- variance analysis for materials and labour costs by product or job
- overheads by type and location
- management accounts in any format the organisation wishes
- customer statements

Obviously this is not an exhaustive list. When evaluating the system, you need to consider the type of business and decide whether the computerised system meets the organisation's information needs or not.

IDENTIFYING THE WEAKNESSES OF THE SYSTEM

The weaknesses in an accounting system often result in **errors** or in **fraud**.

errors and their impact

Errors result from inefficiencies in the internal control system and can cause all sorts of problems, for example:

- an invoice being sent to the wrong customer
- a duplicate invoice being raised
- a discount being incorrectly calculated
- a payment to a supplier being made very late
- an employee being paid the wrong rate of pay
- a customer being sent a formal demand for an overdue account when in fact payment has already been received but entered to the wrong account
- a job being priced incorrectly so the company makes a loss on that sale

You will doubtless be able to add other examples to this list of unfortunate accidents. What these examples have in common is that they result in some form of loss to the organisation involved:

- **loss of money** – when a payment is made for the wrong amount or a discount is incorrectly calculated
- **loss of time** – when a problem has to be sorted out and emails and apologies sent – time is also money, of course
- **loss of reputation** – when customer expectations are not met and the organisation loses face – and even its customer's business

lack of review of procedures and its impact

When a business does not periodically review and update its methods of working, they may become very inefficient, costly to run and delay the production of information. An example of this is set out below.

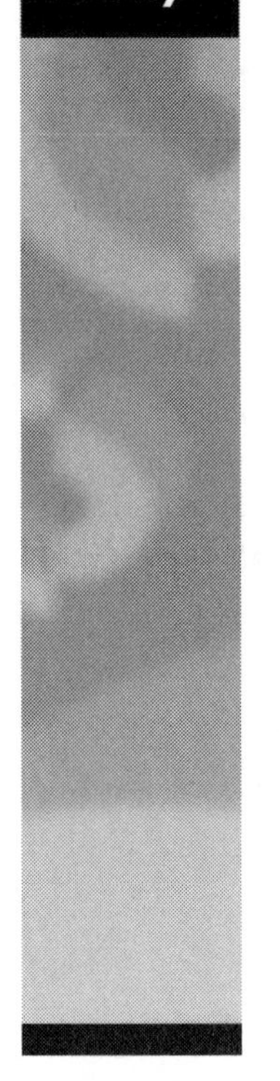

CLEARGLASS WINDOWS LIMITED

situation

A business, ClearGlass Windows Limited, has used Microsoft Excel for the day-to-day management of Accounts Receivable and Accounts Payable for a number of years. The invoices and receipts and payments are then manually entered into a Sales, Purchase and General Ledger, using journals at the end of the month. The monthly management accounts are produced several weeks after month-end.

required

What problems exist in the current system for ClearGlass Windows Limited?

solution

There are several problems with this system:

- data is entered twice – onto Microsoft Excel and an accounting software package, which takes time and money. This is not cost-effective.
- manually entering data is likely to lead to errors in the General Ledger.
- up-to-date information on supplier and customer balances and aged debt will not be available. This could lead to inefficient working practices, where customer debts could be chased once paid or supplier payments might be made twice.
- production of management account information will be slow and it will be unavailable for several weeks.

FRAUD AND ITS IMPACT

Fraud, which was covered in detail in Chapter 4, is another consequence of basic weaknesses in the internal control system of an organisation. It also poses a threat of loss:

- **loss of money** – monetary-based frauds include purchase ledger staff paying fictitious suppliers and diverting the money to their own account, or payroll staff using the same principle to send payroll payments to fictitious employees
- **loss of inventory or revenue** – for example, a case of an employee over-ordering valuable inventory and then stealing it and arranging for its sale at a nearby street market. Or an employee putting cash sales in their own pocket instead of through the till

- **loss of time** – employees do not work the time recorded on time sheets

There are plenty of other examples which could occur in every type of accounting system.

fraud and ethical practices

The opportunity for fraud is closely linked to the ethical standards maintained within the organisation. As part of establishing weaknesses, you will need to look at if there are opportunities for fraud, where controls are weak or do not exist and the lack of ethical principles this allows, for example:

- non-performance of bank reconciliations, which are a key internal control over the cash book and the business's money. They should be performed regularly (weekly or monthly) and any outstanding reconciling items should be followed up. If an employee fails to do this, he or she will be breaking the fundamental principle of professional competence and due care and any fraud being committed may not be found until much later.
- personal expenses claimed through the business by the Sales Director – if there is no authorisation process in place over the Sales Director's expenses, she could put through costs which are personal, rather than just for the business. If this were the case, she would be breaking the fundamental principle of integrity.

As we can see, where weaknesses exist, professional ethics are more likely to be breached, so a strong system of controls will support good ethical practices.

sustainability

Just as weak internal controls will discourage ethical practices, so weak internal controls and procedures in an organisation can discourage sustainable practices too. For example, a lack of selection criteria for suppliers would allow the business to buy from any supplier. Considering suppliers who act in a sustainable manner is much less likely to be a priority when goods are being purchased.

overall system evaluation

As we considered in the previous chapter, it is crucial to understand what a good system looks like and the controls it should have. Internal controls that are missing from the system you are reviewing will allow mistakes or fraud to occur, so you can use this knowledge to 'spot the difference'. The diagram on the next page summarises this process:

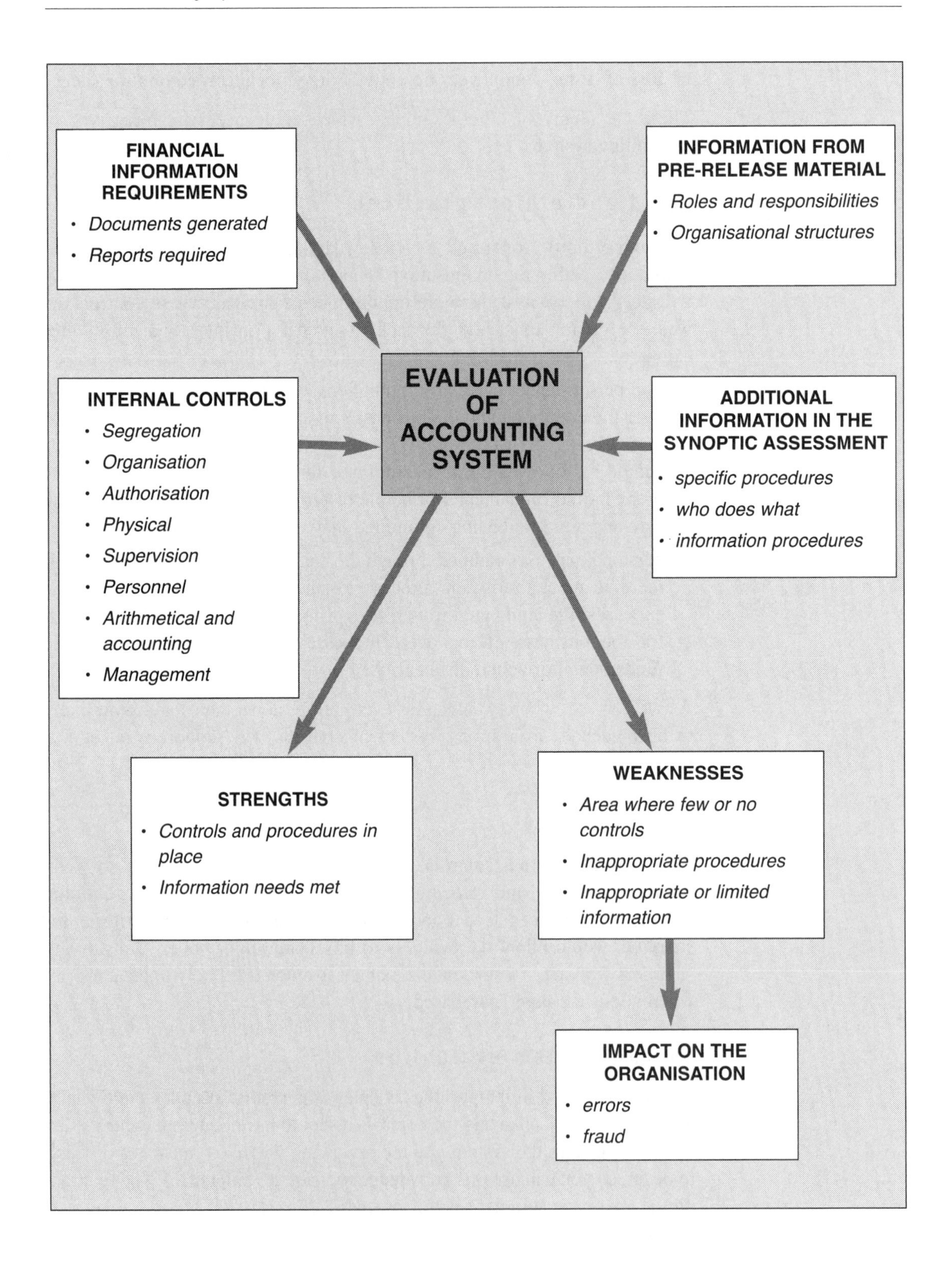
FINANCIAL INFORMATION REQUIREMENTS
• Documents generated
• Reports required
INFORMATION FROM PRE-RELEASE MATERIAL
• Roles and responsibilities
• Organisational structures
EVALUATION OF ACCOUNTING SYSTEM
INTERNAL CONTROLS
• Segregation
• Organisation
• Authorisation
• Physical
• Supervision
• Personnel
• Arithmetical and accounting
• Management
ADDITIONAL INFORMATION IN THE SYNOPTIC ASSESSMENT
• specific procedures
• who does what
• information procedures
STRENGTHS
• Controls and procedures in place
• Information needs met
WEAKNESSES
• Area where few or no controls
• Inappropriate procedures
• Inappropriate or limited information
IMPACT ON THE ORGANISATION
• errors
• fraud

Answering the synoptic assessment

In the synoptic assessment you will be given detailed information regarding an accounting system. You could then be asked to comment on the weaknesses within it and the potential problems that could arise because of this.

examples of weaknesses and the potential problems

You could be asked to review any one of the accounting systems we considered in the previous chapter, namely:

- purchases and cash payment
- revenue and cash receipts
- payroll
- capital expenditure

The costing and inventory system, covered in Chapter 5, is likely to be part of the sales or purchasing system in the synoptic assessment. The following case study indicates the type of information you might be given and the possible weaknesses and potential problems that might arise.

Case Study

DESIGN FOR LIFE LTD: PURCHASING AND CASH PAYMENT SYSTEM

situation

You have been asked to review the adequacy of the controls in Design for Life Ltd's purchasing procedures.

The company operates an integrated accounting system, which includes a purchase accounting module. Matt Arnold, the Purchasing Manager is responsible for managing purchasing activities. The system is organised as follows:

Ordering and receipt

- All purchases must be documented on a pre-numbered purchase order.
- The order should have an agreed price. Andrew Roberts, the Warehouse Manager, can raise an 'emergency order' before a price is agreed if production will be delayed.
- Matt Arnold keeps pre-numbered order books and keeps a record of which department the books are issued to.
- Most Budget Holders keep the order books on their desk.
- Orders for production items are signed off by Andrew Roberts.

- Capital expenditure is signed off by Aneysha Dickson, the Chief Accountant.
- All other purchase orders can be raised by any departmental budget holder, who approve and sign the order.
- The order form is a four-part document. The signed original is sent to the supplier. A green copy is sent to accounts, for Tina Fay, the Accounts Payable Clerk, to file in the Outstanding orders file. The pink and blue copies are then kept by the Budget Holder.
- The goods are delivered to the Budget Holder's location and the Budget Holder sends the blue copy, to Tina Fay as proof it has been delivered. The Budget Holder keeps the pink copy for their files.

New suppliers

- New suppliers are contacted by Matt Arnold. He provides trade references and requests Credit Terms. He also gives them the bank details for Design For Life Ltd.
- The Finance Director, Joseph Armstrong, set the payment terms as 60 days from the end of the month of delivery. Matt Arnold is responsible for communicating these to the supplier. If a supplier suggests a prompt payment discount for early settlement, Matt is able to negotiate this independently.
- Matt has access to the Supplier Standing Data and enters all their information ready for Tina Fay, when she needs to make a payment.

Accounting and paying for purchases

- All purchase invoices are sent to Tina Fay. She checks the calculations, matches the invoice to the blue and green copies of the order held in the Outstanding Orders file and authorises the invoice for payment.
- Tina inputs the invoice onto the computerised accounting system.
- Tina deals with credit notes and queries with suppliers directly, as and when they arise.
- All payments are made using BACS. Aneysha Dickson authorises a payment run each week.

required

(a) Identify systemic weaknesses in the company's internal controls for purchases on credit.

(b) Explain how each weakness could create a problem for the company.

solution

Weakness	Potential problems
No evidence of physical check of quality and quantity of goods.	Goods could be paid for when they have not been received or are of poor quality or are incomplete.
Budget holders and warehouse manager can raise orders and state goods have been received.	Potential fraud – goods could be taken for own use. Goods that are unnecessary for the business could be ordered.
Order books are unsecured.	Potential fraud, as any employee could order goods using the form for buying goods for their own use.
Emergency orders can be made without an agreed price.	The company could pay more for goods than necessary due to the potential lack of negotiation after goods have been delivered.
Only one person authorises orders.	Potential for fraud through collusion with suppliers.
The terms agreed by Matt Arnold are not approved by the Finance Director.	Potential for fraud through collusion with suppliers.
No cash limit for purchase orders.	Large purchases may be made unnecessarily, for a poor price or fraudulently. This could cost the business a lot of money.
Aneysha Dickson authorises payment run.	Potential for fraud through collusion with Tina Fay.
Lack of authorisation of new accounts.	Company may not be buying goods at the best price. Potential for fraud via collusion with suppliers.

Note: We have only considered the weaknesses and their impact on the company. You are not asked to make recommendations in this question!

As you can see from the above Case Study, you will need to very carefully examine what the business is doing in detail, then compare it to the controls and procedures you know should be in the system.

It is particularly important that you understand what documents are created and what they are used for. Does everyone who needs a copy get one? Are documents matched or reviewed to ensure the information is accurate and for the business only? You also need to consider who does what to ensure you correctly identify any weaknesses. Are they are right person to do that procedure? Should they have that level of authority?

purchasing procedures - overheads

The purchases system described for Design for Life Ltd above is for when the business is buying goods. However sometimes the company will incurs costs for which it will be invoiced which are for services and these are most likely to be overhead expenditure. This could include costs such as rent, rates, legal services, photocopier rental, consultancy fees, etc.

The procedures should still include the type of internal controls you would expect within an ordinary purchasing system, such as authorisation of orders, but you will obviously not be able to match orders to Goods Received Notes to ensure goods have been delivered. Therefore you will need to look closely at the controls in place. If the following controls are not in place, you should note them as weaknesses:

authorisation	– Budget holders will be able to order services and they should be of an appropriate level eg managers or senior managers. – These are set authorisation limits, eg Budget holder up to £10,000, Department Director over £10,000. – Budget holders authorise the invoice, using set authorisation limits as before. – Overhead payments are authorised by at least two people eg Finance Director and one other.
segregation	– The Budget Holder or Director authorises the order. – Accounts Payable contact the supplier for payment details. – Payments made are authorised by two appropriate personnel eg one Director and one senior manager.
accounting and arithmetic checks	– Orders will be sequentially numbered and accounts will issue the order number and inform the budget holder of it. – Invoices will be entered onto the invoice register when they come into accounts and will be sequentially numbered, prior to sending to the Budget Holder or Director for authorisation. – Only when invoices are authorised by the appropriate person, are they are posted to the purchase ledger. – All overhead payments made are supported by the invoice and any other supporting documentation.
management	– Management accounts are produced monthly and variances of overhead expenditure are investigated.

commercial impact of weaknesses in the business

The potential problems in the Design For Life Ltd Case Study above were simply the errors that can occur and potential fraud. The business and its trade could also suffer due to current procedures – it may not just be confined to the accounting systems, for example:

- where a business only allows credit applications by post, rather than by email it could be putting obstacles in the way of trade
- where a business only trades through shops and has no online sales facility, it may be losing potential customers

Being more aware of the market the business operates in, its competitors and its products is increasingly important for people working in Finance. We will look at another Case Study to emphasis this point:

Case Study

COOK RIGHT LIMITED: SALES SYSTEM

situation

Cook Right Limited is a small chain of three shops, owned by Paul Goodgrub, specialising in kitchen and cooking equipment. All the shops have been trading for several years.

Sales by shop

- Each shop is staffed by a manager and two assistants. The staff are very knowledgeable about the products Cook Right Limited inventory and they have all worked there for several years.
- Each shop has its own non-digital till, with sales categorised by baking, electrical equipment, utensils and sundry items.
- Each shop also has a credit card machine, which allows Cook Right Limited to take payment using debit and credit cards.
- Cash and credit card sales are recorded separately using the till.
- A till reading is taken at the end of the day and reconciled by the Manager back to the money in the till, allowing for £100 float. Any differences are recorded on the takings sheet.
- The cash is banked every two days, as there are relatively few cash transactions.
- The cash takings sheets and paying-in slips are posted to the Leeds shop, where the bookkeeper is based. This shop acts as the Head Office.

Internet Site

- Cook Right Limited has recently set up an internet site to support the three shops.
- The website contains pictures of a range of current products being stocked.
- Cook Right Limited does not have a computerised inventory currently, so no sales are made using the site.

Accounting for sales

- The takings sheets and till roll information are used to update the general ledger accounts by the bookkeeper, who totals each category of sale. Sales are then recorded using the shop categories only.
- The takings are compared to the bank statements on a monthly basis, when the bank reconciliation is performed. Differences between the takings sheet and the banking or credit card receipts are coded to a suspense account, which is written off to the statement of profit and loss at the end of each year.
- The business owner, Paul Goodgrub reviews the sales information each month and compares it to the previous year's data. Where sales are down, he looks at promotions for the following month to increase sales.

required

(a) Identify the strengths in these procedures for the business. Explain how the business benefits from them.

(b) Identify the weaknesses in these procedures for the business. Explain how these damage the business.

solution

Strengths	**Benefits to the business**
Takings recorded by sales category	The business can see the type of products customers are buying and can monitor margins earned. This may allow it to improve profitability.
Sales information is produced and Paul Goodgrub reviews it each month, compared to last year. Promotions are set for the following month.	Paul Goodgrub is monitoring the level of sales, as the business will need a certain sales level to maintain profitability. Prompt action is taken to drive up sales.
Weaknesses	**Damages the business**
Sales are not recorded in the general ledger by shop.	The business cannot determine which shops are selling particular products well so cannot use this more detailed information to improve profitability further.
Non-digital till is being used	Data regarding sales of individual products is not being collected. More targeted promotions cannot be undertaken. Missed opportunity for sales, as they could be higher.
The internet site is not used to make sales	The business is losing out on internet sales and making it hard for customers to buy, as they must go to the shop to do so.
The inventory system is not computerised	The business may be buying inventory in for one shop when it is available to transfer from another. Impulse sales may be lost, if inventory is not in the location the customer is. Inventory and margins values can only be determined by an inventory count and valuation. Products that are of low profit or that are unprofitable may be stocked ahead of more profitable ones.

solving the problems

It is important to realise that where problems exist, the company must then design appropriate procedures to deal with them, whilst still delivering accounting system requirements. This will be considered in detail in Chapter 7.

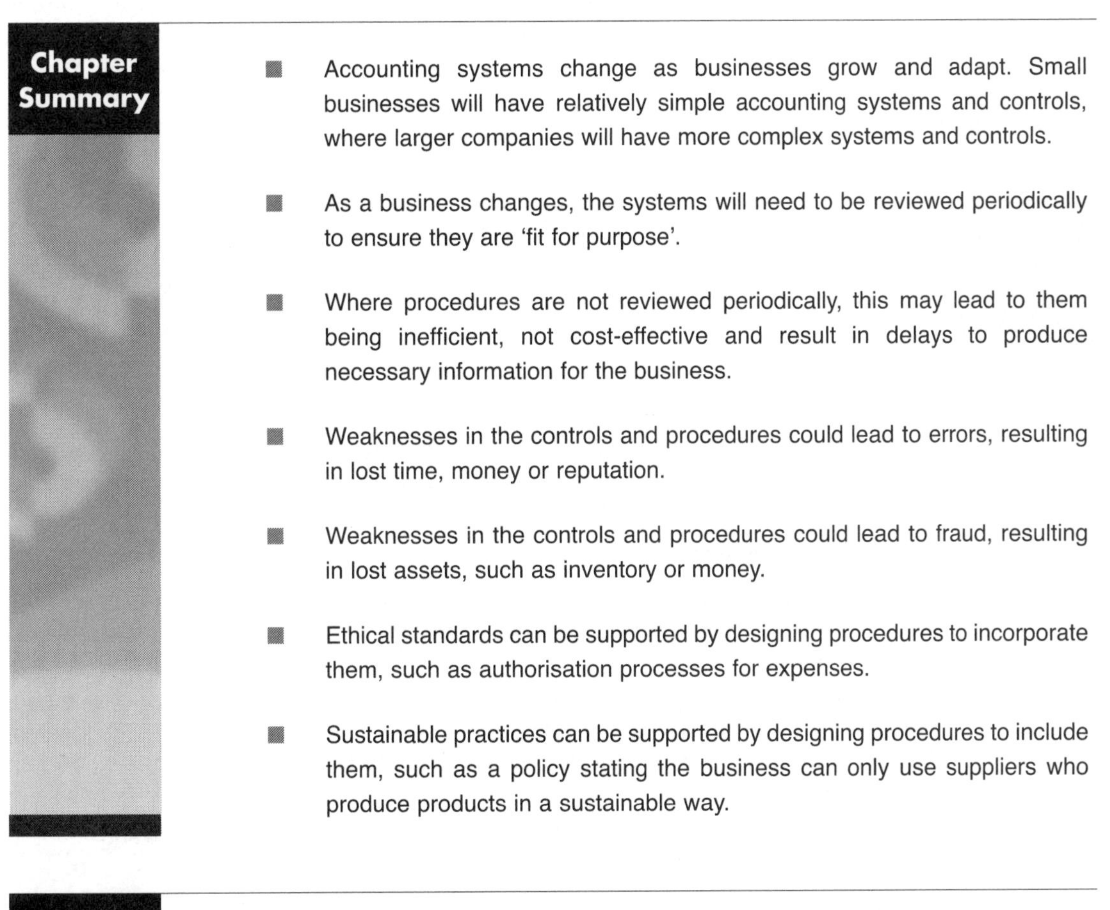

Chapter Summary

- Accounting systems change as businesses grow and adapt. Small businesses will have relatively simple accounting systems and controls, where larger companies will have more complex systems and controls.

- As a business changes, the systems will need to be reviewed periodically to ensure they are 'fit for purpose'.

- Where procedures are not reviewed periodically, this may lead to them being inefficient, not cost-effective and result in delays to produce necessary information for the business.

- Weaknesses in the controls and procedures could lead to errors, resulting in lost time, money or reputation.

- Weaknesses in the controls and procedures could lead to fraud, resulting in lost assets, such as inventory or money.

- Ethical standards can be supported by designing procedures to incorporate them, such as authorisation processes for expenses.

- Sustainable practices can be supported by designing procedures to include them, such as a policy stating the business can only use suppliers who produce products in a sustainable way.

Key Terms

procedure — operating instruction followed by the staff, set out by the organisation eg assessing credit limits for new customers

internal control — activity which prevents or detects errors or omissions occurring in the accounting systems of a business

integrated accounting system — a computerised accounting system where the sales ledger, purchase ledger and cash book automatically update the general ledger

strength a procedure or activity which benefits the business

weakness an area where the business can improve its performance or operation

fraud the use of deception with the intention of obtaining an advantage, avoiding an obligation or causing loss to someone else or to an organisation

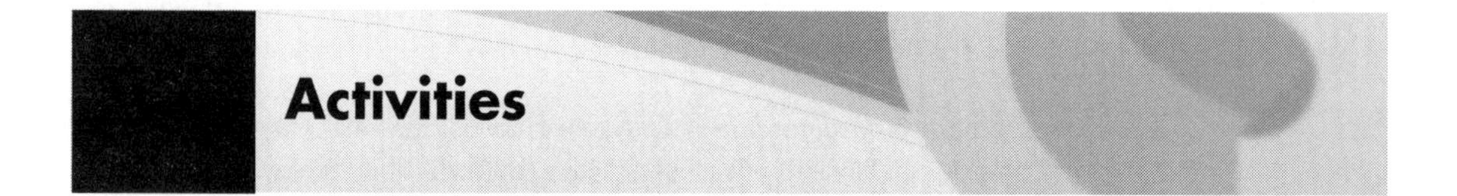

Activities

6.1 Speedy Car Services Limited fits tyres, brakes, batteries and exhausts at 15 branches around the Midlands. The company employs 70 weekly paid staff and 20 salaried staff, who are paid monthly. They have recently, at their Head Office in Walsall, documented their payroll system, set out below:

Inputting hours and amending staff details

- Weekly paid staff complete a timesheet. These are updated in each day by the employee. These are collected together, scanned and emailed to Head Office on a Saturday night by the Branch Manager.
- The Branch Manager completes details of any new starters on a 'Start form'. If the new staff member has a P45, it is attached, along with the employee's bank details. The Branch Manager completes the employment contract. He then sends all of this to HR at Head Office. HR inform the Payroll Clerk.
- The Branch Manager completes a 'Leaver's form' when a staff member leaves and sends it to HR. HR inform the Payroll Clerk.

Payment of wages

- Wages are paid weekly in arrears. The Payroll Clerk at Head Office, inputs the timesheets onto the payroll system.
- Any amendments to standing data are made by the Payroll Clerk. Starters and leavers are amended using the forms sent by the Branch, held by HR.
- The payroll is produced, detailing net pay, deductions and HMRC payments. This is used by the Payroll Clerk to create a cash request.
- The Assistant Accountant at Head Office, reviews the payroll and cash request. He then collects the cash from the bank first thing Thursday morning and the Payroll Clerk makes up the pay packets, including payslips during that day. The cash is sent by courier to the 15 branches late on Thursday for safe-keeping by the manager.
- The Branch Managers distribute the pay packets during Friday to their staff.

Salaries

- Salaried staff are paid monthly by BACS. The payroll is produced by the Payroll Clerk, who also prepares the BACS transfer and the Finance Director authorises the transfer.
- The Finance Director uses Start and Leave forms to authorise starters and leavers, which he gives to HR and the Payroll Clerk.
- Any changes to salaries are authorised by the Finance Director, using an Amendment to Salary form, which he also gives to HR and the Payroll Clerk.
- All statutory deductions are paid by the Assistant Accountant.

Required:

(a) Identify the systemic weaknesses in the company's internal controls for payroll.

(b) Explain how each weakness could create a problem for the company.

6.2 Ashfords Limited hires coaches to businesses and individuals all over the Midlands and North West. It owns a fleet of one hundred and fifty coaches and renews at least twenty of them every year. They have recently employed a new Finance Director, who is keen to ensure capital items are purchased and controlled as efficiently as possible. The following procedures are currently in place for the purchasing of coaches:

Purchase of coaches

- The Maintenance Depot Manager, Keith Wrench, can request to purchase a new coach, when he feels the costs of repairing a vehicle are becoming too high.
- The business has purchased coaches from the same supplier, Comfortable Coaches Limited, for ten years. The owner is a close friend of Mr Ashford, the Managing Director.
- Keith Wrench signs a purchase order, which states the standard price. This price is set at 5% lower than the current list price. A blue copy of the order is sent to the Maintenance Depot, a yellow copy to Accounts and the original to Comfortable Coaches Limited.
- Coaches are purchased outright, not leased. A deposit of 50% is made on order, with the balance due 7 days after delivery.
- They are purchased to a standard specification and Ashfords Limited's branding.
- The coach is delivered to the Maintenance Depot for testing by Keith Wrench. He will sign for delivery, then inspect the coach to ensure there are no problems with it. Where problems occur, Comfortable Coaches Limited will send the relevant personnel to fix the problem.
- The pre-numbered Goods Received Note (GRN) and Delivery Note are both sent to Accounts.
- Coaches are usually put into service within one week of delivery.

Accounting for coaches

- When the Accounts Department receive the yellow order form, they immediately raise a BACS transfer for 50% of the price which is authorised by the Financial Controller. This is recorded in the general ledger as a Prepayment.
- The order is filed in the Coaches Deposit file, waiting for delivery.

- When the Accounts Department receive the GRN, they match it to the yellow copy of the purchase order.
- The invoice is entered onto the Purchase Ledger, once the price has been agreed to the order and it has been checked for accuracy.
- The General Ledger is updated to reflect the new non-current asset.
- The coach details are recorded on a coach spreadsheet, which states the purchase date, supplier, depot location and price. This spreadsheet also contains the depreciation calculations which are used to update the General Ledger.
- The spreadsheet and general ledger are reconciled periodically.

Paying for coaches

- Matching the order to the GRN allows the Purchase Ledger Clerk to authorise the payment to be made.
- The supplier will automatically be paid as part of the weekly payment run one week later.

Disposals

- Keith Wrench is authorised to sell the old coaches.
- He negotiates the price and emails the Accounts Department with the details of the buyer, to enable them to invoice it.
- Terms are strictly 30 days.
- Accounts raise an invoice for the disposal of the coach, according to Keith Wrench's instructions. Ownership information is forwarded once the money has been received.
- The coach spreadsheet and general ledger are updated accordingly with the disposal.

Required:

Identify the weaknesses in the system and the potential problems the business might have because of them.

6.3 First Class Flooring Limited manufacture and sell wooden flooring to independent shops and retailers across the UK. They are based in Woking and employ 150 staff. They produce a range of high quality products using sustainable wood purchased from 30 suppliers across the globe. The company operates an integrated accounting system, which includes a sales module. The Sales Director, Fred Plank, is responsible for a team of four sales staff.

The sales system is explained below:

New customers

- New customers contact First Class Flooring Limited initially via their website or by telephone. They can complete an information request online, which one of the Sales team will use to determine their individual requirements.
- New customers must trade on a cash basis for three months until they are able to set up a credit account.

- The credit assessment process is performed by Alyson Baker, the Credit Controller. A bank reference and two supplier references are requested. Based on this information, Alyson can determine what level of credit to offer.
- Normal credit terms are 30 days from the end of the month.
- The Credit Controller sends reminder letters out at 10 days overdue and 30 days overdue.
- The Credit Controller will then telephone and chase debt by letter and email for up to 90 days overdue before a debt collection agency is involved.

Internet site & promotions

- First Class Flooring Limited has invested heavily in their internet site and it is linked to the sales module and inventory system.
- Customers can complete order requests on line for items held in inventory, viewing product specifications and prices. The ordering system will automatically check if they are within their credit limit and will accept the order if this is the case.
- Alternatively, for non-stock items, they can phone and place the order with one of the sales team, who will review the credit limit for compliance. Some products are made to order, depending on the quality and type of wood being used.
- The company emails out promotional offers on standard products each day, with relevant links to the website to all customers. The software they use reviews items they have purchased in the last three months and tailors the offer accordingly.
- Over 70% of sales are made to existing customers.

Pricing of products

- The business uses a standard costing system for each product.
- The pricing of new products uses the previous month's issues prices, where inventory is recorded using the FIFO system and actual wastage rates from other comparable products.
- Labour rates are based on estimated production time from similar products.
- The overhead absorption rates are historic from last year.
- The list price is generated as fully absorbed cost plus 30% mark-up.
- The Sales Team can give discounts to customers, when authorised by the Sales Director, Fred Plank.

Required:

(a) Identify two key strengths in these procedures. Explain how the business benefits from them.

(b) Identify two key weaknesses in these procedures and explain how they damage the business.

this chapter covers...

In this chapter we will look at the need to make recommendations for improvements to the accounting system. This includes:

- *identifying suitable changes, whether they are due to organisational requirements or statutory changes*
- *changes that are ethical and sustainable*
- *the costs involved in each recommendation and the likely benefits that will follow*
- *problems that might arise during the transitional period*
- *controls needed in the transitional period while changes are implemented*
- *ways to support staff to adapt to the changes*
- *presenting recommendations to management, including the reasons why an organisation should implement them*

MAKING THE RECOMMENDATIONS

A review of an organisation's accounting system will reveal:

- the **strengths** of its internal control system and its method of operating
- the **weaknesses** of the system and the consequent errors that occur, inefficient procedures and opportunities for fraud
- areas of strength and weakness relating to ethical and sustainability issues

Changes may also be needed as the organisation becomes larger and more complex. For example, imagine a manufacturing company is expanding and setting a second factory. The site is 5 miles away from the current factory. New staff and management will be employed to run it. The business will have systems and procedures in place to run a single site, but it will now need to consider issues such as:

- how to collect the information for the new weekly staff, to ensure they are properly paid
- whether to locate accounting staff at one factory or both
- how sales and purchases are going to be recorded at the new site and if the computer systems need to be upgraded to do this efficiently,
- how to restructure the general ledger to allow for detailed analysis of both sites

Changes will therefore be made when the current procedures and systems are no longer 'fit for purpose'.

In the synoptic assessment, you may need to:

- make recommendations for improvement
- justify those recommendations and present them to management
- consider any problems that might occur in the transitional period leading up to the implementation of the new systems

IDENTIFYING SUITABLE CHANGES TO THE ACCOUNTING SYSTEM

You could be asked in the synoptic assessment to make changes in an accounting system where there are weaknesses and potential problems. As we explained in Chapter 6, a weakness exists where controls and procedures that should be there are not present. A recommendation must, therefore, solve the problem and stop the weakness by:

- setting out the new procedures or controls which will resolve the issue – this should be detailed enough for a person reading it to fully understand who is doing what and what documents are involved

- explain the reasons why the business must make the change to the accounting system – this will include benefits to the organisation of making the change. You need to justify to management why the business should be making the change
- be in a format suitable for presenting to management – clearly presented and easy to read

The Case Study that follows leads on from analysis we did in Chapter 6, where we identified problems with the purchasing and payments system of Design for Life Ltd.

Case Study

DESIGN FOR LIFE LTD: PURCHASING AND PAYMENTS SYSTEM

situation

In Chapter 6, on pages 129 to 131 you were asked to review the purchasing system of Design For Life Ltd. You identified the following weaknesses and potential problems resulting from them.

Weakness	Potential problems
No evidence of physical check of quality and quantity of goods.	Goods could be paid for when they have not been received or are of poor quality or are incomplete.
Budget holders and warehouse manager can raise orders and state goods have been received.	Potential fraud – goods could be taken for own use. Goods that are unnecessary for the business could be ordered.
Order books are unsecured.	Potential fraud, as any employee could order goods using the form for buying goods for their own use.
Emergency orders can be made without an agreed price.	The company could pay more for goods than necessary due to the potential lack of negotiation after goods have been delivered.
Only one person authorises orders.	Potential for fraud through collusion with suppliers.
The terms agreed by Matt Arnold are not approved by the Finance Director.	Potential for fraud through collusion with suppliers.
No cash limit for purchase orders.	Large purchases may be made unnecessarily, for a poor price or fraudulently. This could cost the business a lot of money.
Aneysha Dickson authorises payment run.	Potential for fraud through collusion with Tina Fay.
Lack of authorisation of new accounts.	Company may not be buying goods at the best price. Potential for fraud via collusion with suppliers.

required

Recommend suitable changes to be made to the accounting system to resolve each of the weaknesses. Explain the benefit for each recommendation, including any assumptions you make.

solution

Recommendation	Benefit and assumptions
Produce a written Goods Received Procedure, which includes inspecting the goods, comparing it to the order and signing the Delivery Note and Goods Received Note (GRN) as proof of the check, noting where anything is damaged or short-ordered, prior to the GRN being sent to Accounts. Only authorised staff should receive goods. Train all staff in this procedure.	Goods will only be paid for if they have been received in good condition and complete. Assume staff will continue to match GRN and the order correctly.
Orders should be authorised by two people, one of whom is a senior member of staff eg a Director.	Staff will be unable to order goods for their own use and receive them when they come in. Purchases information in the financial statements will only include items purchased for the business. The risk of potential fraud will be reduced.
All order books should be locked away securely by Budget Holders.	The risk of fraud, where employees purchase goods for themselves, will be reduced.
All orders, including emergency orders, cannot be authorised unless they include a price.	The company will pay a negotiated price for goods. The price will be competitive, so the organisation's profitability will be maintained.
Two people must authorise an order (as above).	Goods will only be purchased for the business at an agreed price. The potential for fraud through collusion with suppliers is removed.
Where payments terms differ to those set as required by the Finance Director, they must be approved by the Finance Director prior to being agreed with the supplier.	The Finance Director will be aware of suppliers where different credit terms need to be met. The Finance Director will be able to monitor and budget cash flow more efficiently. The potential for fraud through collusion with suppliers is reduced.
Orders must be authorised by two people, one of whom is a senior manager or Director.	Large purchases will not be made unnecessarily, for a poor price or fraudulently. The profitability of the business will be maintained.
Two people need to authorise the payment run, including one director. There must be supporting documentation with payments.	The business will not make payments unnecessarily. The potential for fraud is reduced. Assume the supporting documentation will be reviewed when the payment run is authorised.
All new accounts should be authorised by the Production Director.	The company will be buying goods at the best price. The potential for fraud through collusion with suppliers is removed.

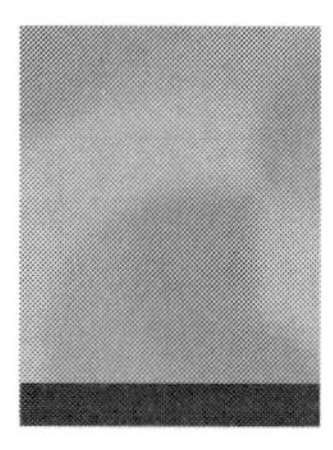

The recommendations can be beneficial for a number of reasons including:

- they reduce the likelihood of fraud or error occurring
- they make the process more efficient, resulting in time or cost savings
- they will improve customer service and therefore improved reputation of the business

THE IMPACT OF CHANGES ON OPERATING PROCEDURES

Many of the changes suggested in the purchases system for Design For Life Ltd would have cost little to implement and would have had a relatively small impact on the day to day operations.

One area which would have changed significantly was the new Goods Received Procedure. To be effective, it would have to be clearly written and staff would need to be thoroughly trained, especially in procedures when goods are damaged or incomplete. The time taken to receive goods would increase considerably.

Sometimes, one recommended change can have an impact across much of an organisation. The following example illustrates where a change in one area can have implications for almost all the organisation.

Case Study

COOK RIGHT LIMITED: CHANGE TO TILL SYSTEM

situation

The business, Cook Right Limited, has a chain of three shops, specialising in selling kitchen equipment, all of which have been trading for several years. Each shop is staffed by three people who have been employed for several years. The current systems are in place:

- The sales recording is by a non-digital till in each shop and the sales are recorded categorised by baking, electrical equipment, utensils and sundry items.
- The shops can take payment by cash, debit card and credit card.
- Cash taking are recorded daily on a takings sheet by the Shop Manager. The cash and credit card payments are reconciled at the end of the day to the till roll. Differences are noted on a takings sheet.
- The takings sheets and paying in slips are posted to the Leeds shop, which acts as a Head Office.
- Sales are recorded by category in the general ledger. The bookkeeper adds all the takings sheets together and records each category in total, not by shop. The bookkeeper therefore enters the cash and credit card information manually into the general ledger.
- Currently there is no computerised inventory system.
- Paul Goodgrub, the owner, reviews sales information each month and compares it to the previous year's data. Where sales in a category are down, he proposes promotions for the following month to boost sales.

required

The owner Paul Goodgrub, is considering updating the tills in all three shops. Recommend how he could update the system to improve sales and reporting information. State the benefits of the new system and any assumptions you make.

solution

Recommendation

Paul Goodgrub could invest in an Electronic Point of Sales system (EPOS) for each of the three shops.

The benefits of the system would be:

- Accurate product by product sales data by shop, which could automatically update the general ledger at the end of the day.
- Potential to computerise inventory, allowing accurate margin analysis on a product by product basis. This would also mean better inventory control and ordering across the shops.
- More focused promotions on products to increase sales.
- Quicker identification of slow moving items and ability to take appropriate action.
- Paul Goodgrub can have access to accurate sales information in 'real time' without delay due to waiting for takings sheets to be sent through.

Assumptions

- Cost of EPOS system is acceptable to Paul Goodgrub compared to the benefits it brings
- Staff are willing to be trained on a more complex system and will enter the data correctly. The training cost will need to be paid.
- Bookkeeper can be adequately trained to ensure the data from the EPOS system reconciles back to the takings accurately and reliably. There may be an initial cost.
- General ledger can be set up to include more complex reporting data. If not, the business may need to reconfigure its general ledger. There will be associated costs.
- All management reporting will need to be set up for the new data. There will be associated costs.
- EPOS software can be integrated with the general ledger.

conclusion

The new till system is not simply a different way of recording the data. The operating procedures for staff and the bookkeeper will all change significantly and it will take time to implement. Management always need to consider how cost effective the changes being suggested are – do the costs outweigh the benefit?

HOW MUCH WILL IT ALL COST?

Where any changes are required, the organisation will inevitably incur additional costs. For example, extra costs may be incurred in employing more staff, training staff or acquiring new computer systems. An example cost analysis is shown below.

cost analysis – a practical example

Installation of a new computer system in the Accounts Department

An estimate of the likely costs is as follows:

	£
– the cost of the hardware	10,000
– the cost of the software	5,000
– the installation cost	2,500
– the cost of training the staff (see next table)	3,790
– annual maintenance cost	1,750
– insurance of hardware and for loss of data	1,250
	24,290

When working out a statement of costs you should show how you arrived at the **training costs**. These costs include the cost of the time spent training by the employees of the organisation which would otherwise have been spent in productive work. A typical calculation might look like this:

	£
time spent by a manager in training	
20 hours x £50 per hour	1,000
plus 15% on employer costs (National Insurance etc)	150
time spent by 8 assistants in training	
20 hours x 8 x £10 per hour	1,600
plus 15% on employer costs (National Insurance etc)	240
time spent by external trainer	
20 hours x £40 per hour	800
TOTAL TRAINING COST	3,790

cost-benefit analysis

Cost-benefit analysis compares the amount of resources used (which are measured in money terms) with the benefits obtained from a project (which are not always measurable in money terms).

We have already considered the cost of a new system in the above example.

On the 'benefit' side you will need to analyse the benefits from a project that cannot be measured in financial terms, for example:

- better communication links between staff
- an improvement in the quality of a service provided to clients/customers
- a more effective reporting system

Cost-benefit analysis tells you whether the benefits will outweigh the costs.

assessing the benefits

You may well ask 'How can these costs benefit the organisation?'

Sometimes the benefit will result in cost savings, although this is difficult to quantify in your recommendations.

A new computerised system means that money savings can be made in the way the system operates, for example:

- many routine operations will be speeded up which will save time and therefore reduce the wages bill
- electronic statements of account to customers will save on postage
- electronic payments to suppliers will also save time and money
- computer printed invoices will have fewer errors and therefore save time and money

If you are required to cost the savings you will be given some information to help you, eg time spent on current procedures. Where you do have to make assumptions you need to state what they are, eg pay rate, time saved.

There are also benefits which cannot be quantified in terms of money:

- the organisation will appear more professional
- the service provided by the organisation will be more efficient, which means that there will be fewer errors and problems, all of which cost time and money

cost saving – an example

Cost saving from a new computer system in the Accounts Department

	£
Time saved inputting data manually from Excel per week	100
(10 hours x £10 per hour plus 15% on employees costs)	15
	115
Yearly saving 52 x 115	5,980

conclusion

In conclusion, you will see that the benefits which emerge from a cost-benefit analysis cannot always be given a monetary value. The final decision must rest on the evidence of all the benefits provided – in basic terms "will it significantly improve the accounting system and is it worth all the money?"

OTHER CONSIDERATIONS

ethical principles

When you are making recommendations, you always need to consider the ethical implications of your suggestions. As a member of the AAT you are bound by the AAT Code of Ethics. Therefore you need to consider how the recommendations you make in the synoptic assessment support the following ethics, which have been considered previously in Chapter 5:

- objectivity
- professional behaviour
- professional competence and due care
- integrity
- confidentiality

For example,

- **objectivity** – paying staff in the same job a different wage, depending on if you are friends with them
- **professional behaviour** – using abusive language in emails
- **professional competence and due care** – rushing a management report and not checking it thoroughly, as you want to go on holiday

- **integrity** – informing your manager you have completed a job when you have not
- **confidentiality** – telling a customer the profit being made on their jobs

It is good practice to evaluate recommendations against ethical principles to ensure they are supported.

sustainable principles

Where possible, recommendations should also support one or more of the three sustainable principles:

- **economic growth** – increasing long-term company profits to benefit employees by using fair pricing policies or pricing agreements with preferred suppliers
- **environmental protection** – conserving the environment and resources by moving to a paperless integrated purchasing system will reduce paper use
- **social equality** – considering the social well being of people locally and worldwide, by employing apprentices and training staff in suitable qualifications to benefit the organisations and the individuals

corporate social responsibility

The organisation you are given may have its own internal corporate social responsibility (CSR) document. Often these are produced by large organisations and will formalise many sustainable practices. Examples of CSR initiatives are:

- sourcing products from renewable sources and where local economies benefit
- ensuring suppliers are supported in sustainable development activities and are treated respectfully
- fund raising activities by staff and customers for charitable causes
- carbon neutral production plants and warehousing
- reducing waste by redesigning packaging

Answering the synoptic assessment

When asked to offer recommendations, you may not specifically be asked in the requirement to consider ethical and sustainable issues. However, you should include them, particularly when asked to justify why the recommendation should be made.

SWOT ANALYSIS

A useful analytical tool to help bring together the analysis of the current system and what a business could do in the future is a SWOT analysis, where the organisation analyses its Strengths, Weaknesses, Opportunities and Threats for a particular situation or system. We will now look at each of these areas in turn.

Strengths

These are the areas in the organisation where it is currently operating effectively and efficiently and where it is already good at what it does. This could be internal or seen from the point of suppliers or customers. Examples of the kind of areas that you could consider as strengths are:

- good procedures controlling particular parts of the business eg excellent Credit Control
- the service suppliers receive – eg prompt, accurate payment
- capable, qualified people
- efficient goods despatch procedures so the correct goods are sent to the customer
- IT systems and procedures which meet the needs of the business and ensure the quality and timeliness of data
- strong ethical and sustainable practices supported by management

Weaknesses

These are areas of the organisation or activities where the level of achievement is low. These could be apparent from within the business or be made known from the opinions of customers, employees or suppliers. You have examined at weaknesses in systems in Chapter 6. The SWOT analysis can highlight these weaknesses:

- a poor sales system, where customers are chased for payment for invoices they have already paid
- unqualified or inadequate personnel to process information, leading to errors in reporting and decision making data
- a non-integrated accounting system
- an inadequate system for recording cash sales
- an ineffective internet site, which customers cannot easily navigate – this will not encourage them to make purchases
- inadequate or inappropriate sales ordering processes

Essentially you are looking for areas the organisation can improve.

Opportunities

The business should consider how it can improve its internal controls and operating procedures. Again, this could benefit customers or suppliers. Examples include:

- installing new IT systems to integrate ledgers and make reporting more timely
- an improved internet site to generate future sales and profits
- implementing a paperless purchasing system, to provide a more efficient service to suppliers
- implementing new electronic sales initiatives to improve customer service and sales, and reduce marketing cost

Threats

Finally, threats are obstacles the business faces in its current environment. Threats could arise for many different reasons, for example, potential problems with customers or competitors. They could also arise through changes in technology or the environment in which the business operates. Examples include:

- competitors launching new and more attractive products
- over-reliance on customers or specific contracts
- changes in technology making it harder to compete
- demand in the market for the products of the business
- over-reliance on specialist suppliers
- the pace of change in the market

HOW CHANGE AFFECTS STAFF WHO USE THE SYSTEMS

supporting staff through changes in accounting systems

Any significant change in the accounting system will clearly impact on the staff involved. They will feel challenged, and perhaps threatened.

Part of any recommendation for change should include a plan for ensuring that the staff will acquire the necessary skills and knowledge so that they can use the revised system effectively. For example, where a new or updated computer system is recommended. This could include:

- internal training courses and external training courses
- 'teach-yourself' facilities such as manuals, DVDs, online tutorials and the 'Help' menus provided with the computer software
- telephone support lines made available by the software provider (Sage, for example, provide an excellent 'helpline')

Staff training can be an expensive item and should form a prominent element in the cost-benefit analysis (see below) which assesses the total costs of a recommendation against the benefits provided.

changes to organisational procedures

Recommendations may include other modifications to the internal control system which will impact on staff because they will change everyday procedures. For example:

- improvements to credit control procedures, eg credit references on new customers
- improvements to payment procedures, eg sending of BACS payments and Faster Payments to suppliers
- increased security of cash handling, eg having two people to check tills
- increased password security, eg changing passwords regularly
- stricter procedures relating to confidentiality (a fundamental ethical principle)

These changes would need to be communicated to staff, incorporated in the procedures of the accounting system, and monitored on a regular basis.

changes to external regulations

Changes to external regulations may also mean that the staff need to amend working practices, to ensure they continue to comply with the statutory regulations ie legislation and also the accounting standards. Examples include:

- Taxation regulations affecting areas such as:

  – PAYE for individuals on payroll, income tax, National Insurance and other deductions. When real time reporting was introduced by HMRC, payroll staff needed to ensure payroll was being produced accurately and promptly enough to allow them to comply. This will have changed the collection and processing of data in many organisations.

  – VAT – if VAT rates change for certain types of items, such as energy for example, the accounting staff may need to review the methods of coding and processing purchase invoices, to ensure the new correct amount of VAT is claimed back. There may also need to be amendments to the standing data for these suppliers and new VAT rate set up on the accounting system.

- Company law – set out in the Companies Act 2006 – requires that company financial statements (of larger companies) should be audited; these statements are drawn up in a set format and sent to shareholders. Where the format of the accounts is changed or updated, the organisation will need to review its reporting and accounting practices to ensure the data it collects will enable it to comply with this legislation.
- International Accounting Standards – these are often updated to reflect changes in the requirements of users of the accounts. Where changes occur, the staff may need to make changes to the accounts within the general ledger, for example, to collect additional information, so the financial statements can comply with the new International Accounting Standard.
- Data protection law – set out in the Data Protection Act 1998 – protects data, including financial data, relating to individual customers. There should be strict policies over the protection of data for payroll, customers and suppliers. Any changes to this law, such as an decrease in the length of time the organisation can keep information for, could mean the payroll, customer and supplier databases would need a review policy put in place.

MOVING FROM ONE SYSTEM TO ANOTHER

problems that might occur

Inevitably, there will be a 'transition period' moving from system of operation to another where employees are familiar with the current methods of working but need to learn and implement the new methods. It may simply be a new Credit control policy for new customers, which affects the Credit Controller alone, or it could be the introduction of a completely new integrated computerised accounting system. Whatever the change is, you need to consider the problems that could arise in this transition period.

- Integrity and capture of data – data could be lost or transferred incorrectly.
- Controls may cease to operate or be less effective eg Credit Control may not occur as the staff are busy transferring data, rather than chasing customers for payment.
- The service given to customers and suppliers could be adversely affected – Accounts Receivable may be taking longer to deal with queries if running on two systems temporarily or they could chase debts already paid incorrectly.

- Staff may be demotivated and unwilling to engage with the changes required for the business – this will make implementing a new system more difficult and possibly take a lot longer than expected.

control of a transition

To ensure the changes are implemented smoothly and the new system works, the organisation could implement the following:

- **Dual or parallel running** – where a complete system, say a new sales ledger is being installed, the business could input all the data onto both the new and old system for a period of time, to ensure the new system is working correctly. The two systems must be reconciled and any differences investigated and resolved prior to the old system being run down and turned off.
- **Test databases** – often a business will test new software in the 'test' part of the current system to ensure it works properly. They may input data which tested the controls within it eg authorisation limits, to see if they work properly. They will then swap systems once they are confident they work as expected. The information moved over from the old system to the new will need to be reconciled.
- **Phased implementation** – rather than overwhelm staff with changes, a business could implement them in a phased way ie one new system or process at a time. For example, rather than implement an entire integrated purchasing system, they could implement purchase ordering, followed by a new purchase ledger, then the new cash payments system. As each system is implemented, the staff and management review it and agree when it is working as it should and they are ready for the next phase. Any data transferred between the old and new will need to be reconciled.
- **Piloting changes** – to see if the new procedures will work effectively, the business could pilot them in certain areas. If it has several locations or companies, the new procedures could be put in place in one location to see where problems may arise. These issues can be resolved prior to it being 'rolled out' to the rest of the business. For example, a new Credit Assessment procedure for new customers could be trialled for three months at one organisation to see if it is better than the current procedure.

To ensure the process is properly controlled, the staff must be sufficiently trained prior to the change in the system or procedure, rather than after it. The staff will be, no doubt, be worried about working in a different way. By training them beforehand, they will be able to inform management of any areas they believe will be difficult to implement or more costly than management expect. They are also more likely to co-operate if they feel involved in the process at an early stage.

If the system change is significant, the business should consider how to manage any potential impact on customers or suppliers where they could be affected. For example, where a new payments system is being installed, the business may choose to pay some invoices early to minimise any potential impact on the supplier's cash flow. If there were any problems during the implementation, this could lead to delays to payments, and by paying early the business would have more time to resolve the issue.

Answering the synoptic assessment

It is likely that you will be given one area of the accounting system to focus on, such as the sales system. You will be given the current operating procedures, which have weaknesses within them and may have to consider whether they are commercially damaging to the business and cause problems. Any recommendations you make will need to limit or stop the damage to the business or solve the problem.

Chapter Summary

- An organisation's requirements of the accounting system change over time as the organisation develops so all systems should be periodically reviewed to ensure they are 'fit for purpose'.
- Any changes to the system or procedures must be suitable for the organisation in terms of reducing the likelihood of fraud or errors, making the process more efficient or improving the service given and therefore reputation of the business.
- Where recommendations are made, the benefits to the organisation should be explained, as well as the likely costs associated with them and how these are arrived at, so that management can justify the change.
- Any changes are likely to have an impact on the staff in the organisation. They may need additional training and support during this period of change.
- Staff may also need to change accounting systems and working practices when statutory regulations or organisational requirements change.
- Problems may occur as procedures or systems move from an old to a new system. The service to customers and suppliers may be disrupted, staff may find the changeover difficult and demotivating and the data which is moved across may have errors within it.

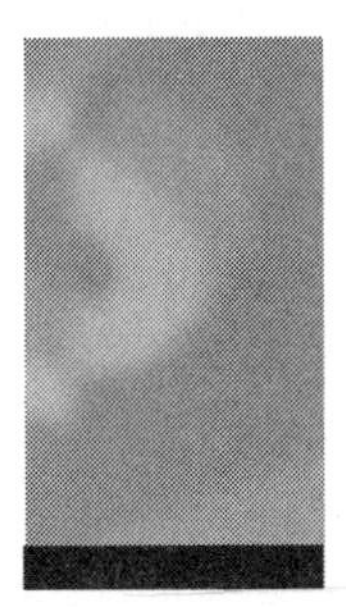

- Controls should be put in place to minimise the likelihood of these problems occurring, including staff involvement and training, communication with customers and suppliers, controls over the transfer of data. New systems should be implemented in a planned manner.
- Where changes are suggested, recommendations should consider their ethical and sustainable impact and support these.

Key Terms

fit for purpose — the system will do the job it was designed to do efficiently

SWOT analysis — an analytical tool to consider the strengths, weakness, opportunities and threats of a business and its procedures

transition period — the period where an organisation moves from an old accounting system, or part of an accounting system to a new one

statutory regulations — the laws, set by Parliament, which the organisation must comply with

cost benefit analysis — the comparison of the amount of monetary resources used with the benefits obtained from a project

Activities

7.1 Travel America Limited is a travel agency that arranges holidays in the USA. It has five outlets in locations around the country as well as a call centre in Birmingham. The company specialises in tailor-made holidays for independent travellers. It has experienced tough competition in the last few years as the internet has eroded the lower margin side of its business. It is now focused on customers who travel First or Business Class, who will pay to experience 'unique moments' on their holidays. Many customers are repeat business.

You have been asked to review the purchases system and make recommendations for improvement.

Ordering and booking

- Bookings generally consist of flights, accommodation, trips and tours.
- Every holiday is individually costed using the hotel rates and margin information that is loaded into the contracts side of the Reservations System.
- Budgeted US dollar requirements are entered in the accounting system for the year by fixing the currency exchange rate in advance. This protects Travel America limited from significant exchange rate fluctuations.
- The exchange rate is set in the system for the year and dollars purchased in advance to set the rate.
- The Reservations system automatically emails a request to the hotel for the accommodation.
- Each day, the Sales Manager of each outlet reviews the email confirmations and gives them to the sales consultant to update the status to 'Confirmed' in the system.
- Flights are purchased using an online booking engine. The sales consultant searches and finds a flight, then reserves it for the customer. The airline booking engine automatically updates the cost information in the Reservations system. The Reservations system applies the appropriate margin for that fare to give the customer a price. All flight costs are in Sterling.
- Tours are booked on a 'Request basis' using the cost and margin information in the Reservations system via automatic email. They are confirmed in the same way as the hotels.
- Customers pay a 10% deposit on booking and the balance is due eight weeks prior to departure from the UK.

Suppliers

- Travel America Limited deals with luxury hotels and tours, so they have contracts with most of their suppliers, at fixed hotel rates.
- Where a new supplier is required, Travel America will initially request 30 days credit, supplying recent financial information, bank references and references from key suppliers. Often this will secure credit. If not, they will request to pay 10% deposit and full payment on arrival date.

- Travel America has contracts with all airlines that fly to the USA. The airline tickets are paid for using the BSP system, where airlines submit electronic data by ticket and agent to a centralised agency, who then collect payment from the agent for all the airlines they contract with.

Accounting for and paying for purchases

- Costs are held on a booking by booking basis within the Reservations system.
- The Reservations system has an integrated purchase ledger, where all hotel and tour suppliers' accounts are held.
- Payment terms for each supplier are loaded into the Reservations system.
- Payments for hotels and tours are made in US dollars, according to credit terms, using the Reservations system. The booking is updated with the payment and costs correctly updated accordingly.
- The Accounts Payable Team generates payments and completes the payment run information.
- A payments run is made each week. The Financial Controller authorises the BACS payment.
- Flight payment data is downloaded from the Reservations system and compared to the file of payments due from BSP each month on the first of the month. The BSP payment information is then uploaded back into the payments part of the purchase ledger of the Reservations System. BSP is taken automatically seven days after Travel America receives the file ie 8th of the month. Flights are requested by BSP four weeks prior to travel.
- The Reservations system generates a journal each month which states the purchases made, by type – flights, hotels, tours, insurance – and the cash paid.
- This is used to update the general ledger.
- The supplier payments are reconciled to the US dollar and UK cash book during the next month.

Required:

You are required to identify four features of these procedures: one strength one weakness one opportunity and one threat.

- Identify a strength and explain how the business benefits from this.
- Identify a weakness in these procedures. Explain how this damages the business and suggest a remedy.
- Identify an opportunity to improve the procedure, explaining how the procedures should be changed and how the business could benefit.
- Identify one threat to the effectiveness of these procedures. Explain how this can damage the business and suggest an action that would reduce the risk.

7.2 Best Bathrooms Limited make and sell baths, sinks and sanitary ware to retailers and online. They have several well established product lines, which they carry in inventory. They have a factory in Cardiff and employ 85 people. They currently deal with 300 regular customers, who account for 70% of their sales. They have been trading for several years.

You have been asked to carry out a review of their sales order processing and despatch procedures and make recommendations for improvement.

You have interviewed the Sales Director (Jacob Dyer), Finance Director (Andy Clarke), Credit Controller (Tracey Misham), Warehouse Manager (Dave Stokeley) and Accounts Receivable Clerk (Jayne Grey). Your findings are below:

Sales ordering

- Customers are able to order a current catalogue over the phone or view it as a pdf file online, using the internet site.
- Order forms can be completed online to be processed by the Sales Department.
- Orders are pre-numbered sequential documents.
- The Sales Department will contact the customer within 48 hours to confirm the order, price and delivery date. Sales staff can discount the list price to close the sale.
- The order will be printed off three times. The original order will be emailed back to the customer, sales retain the blue copy and the pink copy goes to Dave Stokeley.

New customers

- Retail customers can apply for credit. They must provide two years' accounts, two supplier references and a bank reference. Tracey Misham will use a credit agency and the information provided to set a credit limit, authorised by Andy Clarke.
- Online customers must pay using PayPal or by direct transfer through the bank. Jayne Grey will email the Warehouse that payment has been made.
- Credit terms are 30 days and are all authorised by Andy Clarke.

Despatch procedures

- Dave Stokeley reviews the outstanding orders file daily to ensure no items are waiting to be despatched for longer than a few days.
- The Warehouse take the order form the file and 'pick' the items on it from the shelf or location in the warehouse and box them or pallet them ready for despatch.
- A three part pre-numbered Goods Despatched Note (GDN) is generated and signed by the warehouse staff to confirm the condition of the goods. One copy is attached to the order and these are both sent to Accounts, who will use them to raise the invoice. Two are sent with the Delivery Team.
- The customer signs for the Goods and keeps one copy of the GDN. The signed copy comes back to Best Bathrooms Limited as proof of delivery and is filed in the Proof of Delivery file in the Warehouse.

Required:

Make recommendations to the internal controls and procedures of Best Bathroom Limited's sales ordering, new customer and despatch procedures and explain the benefits to the business.

7.3 Regal Hotel Limited own a chain of hotels in the Cotswolds. They have been trading very successfully for several years. Their accounts department is based in Evesham. They employ 70 permanent staff and use casual staff in the Summer months, their peak season, to cope with the additional customers and their needs. There is an Area Manager, who oversees the Hotel Managers.

You have been asked to review the payroll system and make recommendations for its improvement.

Starters and leavers

- Each hotel manager is authorised to advertise for any staff, including casual, short-term contracted staff, when needed.
- The Hotels tend to employ staff who have experience and they are often not from the local area. The turnover of casual staff is very high.
- Weekly paid staff are given contracts that are 'zero–hours' contracts, where shifts are not guaranteed.
- The Manager completes a 'New starter form' and fills out the standard temporary contract, completing the hourly rate as per the Head Office rates schedule. This is based on age and experience.
- The Manager also completes the employee details, including bank details. Both parties sign it.
- The employee must provide evidence of their right to work in the UK.
- All this information is sent to Head Office to verify and input into the payroll system.
- Leavers sign a 'Leavers form', authorised by the Hotel Manager. This is sent to HR, who confirm details to the Payroll Clerk.
- The Financial Controller is informed of all leavers and confirms they have been removed from the payroll.

Weekly and monthly payroll

- All staff have to clock in and clock out, using a swipe card each day. This payroll system records their working hours.
- The Manager is usually there at the start of the shift five days out of seven.
- Where staff work longer than 40 hours per week, they will be paid overtime at basic rate plus a half. During the Summer, this frequently happens, as casual staff tend to 'come and go'.
- The Payroll Clerk who works in the Evesham Head Office takes the information from the clocking in systems and manually enters each person's hours and overtime into a payroll system. This takes approximately three hours each week. The Payroll Clerk is paid £15 per hour.
- The system calculates appropriate deductions and generates weekly pay slips.
- The Payroll Clerk uses this to generate a weekly BACS request. The BACS request is authorised by the Financial Controller.
- All other staff are paid monthly. The procedures for recruitment are all controlled by HR at Head Office, except for the interview process. The Managing Director signs off all new monthly paid staff.

- The monthly payroll is processed by the Payroll Clerk and generates the BACS report. The BACS request is authorised by the Financial Controller.

Required:

(a) Identify weaknesses in the internal procedures within the business, the problems they could cause and make recommendations to resolve them.

(b) The business has investigated integrating the payroll system with the clocking in system. The integration software will cost £500. The Financial Controller has asked you to prepare a Cost Benefit Analysis for the integration.

(c) Identify the problems that could occur with the change in system and suggest actions you can take to limit them.

Answers to chapter activities

CHAPTER 2: THE ACCOUNTING FUNCTION – HOW IT WORKS

2.1 (b) The directors of the company

2.2 **(a)** Invoicing sales, collecting money from customers, travel expenses, paying staff, room hire, website fees, mobile phones costs. The main accounting functions would be payroll, sales ledger and purchase ledger.

(b) A flat structure. As both owners are involved in the business and it has few employees, you would expect there to be few layers of management within it. All the recruiters would probably report to one of the owners and there would only be few support staff, the main one being the accountant.

2.3 **(a)** Invoicing, collecting money from customers, paying staff, costing, paying suppliers and factory overheads. The main accounting functions would be costing, payroll, purchase ledger, sales ledger and cashier.

(b) A hierarchical structure. As the business has two divisions , with many staff, the business would need several layers of management to control production, distribution and selling the products.

2.4 **(a)** A hierarchical structure. Due to the size and complexity of the business and its geographical spread, the company will need many different management and employee roles to allow it to operate efficiently, effectively and safely. It will need to have a Board of Directors who are accountable for specific areas, then a team under each of them to deliver in those areas.

(b)

EMAIL

To: All Payroll staff

From: Charlotte Churchill, Payroll Manager

Cc: Finance Director

Subject: Change in income tax rates and treatment of travel discounts

Payroll staff

As you may know, the tax rates on wages and salaries are due to change on 6 April 20-2. The payroll system should automatically be updated for the new rates and personal allowances. However, to ensure it is working correctly, you must manually calculate a sample of net wages calculations and agree it to the system. Any errors must be reported to me immediately.

The rules for travel discounts have also been changed and any staff who are given a discount must be taxed accordingly. An additional amount must be calculated reflecting the value of the discount and added to their wages or salary, to be subject to tax as if it were salary.

Human Resources

You need to email to all managers to ensure they inform all staff that the tax rates are changing this month and to contact payroll if they have any queries with their wage deductions. You must also circulate the new rules for taxing discounts given as part of normal pay, to ensure staff are aware of the change.

2.5 (d) All of the Directors – The Directors run the business together, so legally they are all responsible if the company does not comply with changes in legislation.

CHAPTER 3: STAKEHOLDERS AND THEIR INFORMATION NEEDS

3.1 **(a)** The bank is a key external stakeholder. The business needs to be able to meet any terms of the loan and also to be able to make repayments and pay the finance charges each year.

The bank may need information such as quarterly management accounts to monitor profitability and cash flow.

The parts supplier is a key external stakeholder. It is important that Speedy Car Services Limited is able to fit whatever a customer requires, as much of the trade is walk in, rather than booked in advance. If the business cannot provide the tyre or part required they are likely to lose the sale.

The supplier is likely to have given credit terms to Speedy Car Services Limited. They will require yearly financial accounts to monitor the businesses cash flow and ability to repay debts on time, as per the agreed credit terms.

The Government is a key stakeholder, as they want the business to trade and employee staff and pay income taxes, company taxes and VAT.

The Government will want to see the financial statements to determine the profits generated by the business and so their likely tax revenue.

The employees are key internal stakeholders. They have worked for the business for several years and .are likely to have pensions through it.

The employees are unlikely to have access to the financial accounts. If they work to bonuses, they are likely to want to see weekly and monthly sales figures to allow them to calculate their bonuses.

(b) The owners are likely to use the following key performance indicators:

- Gross profit margin %, by product and branch
- Weekly sales figures by branch and product
- Parts wastage % (Value of wasted parts/ total parts purchased) x 100
- Labour % (Labour cost as a percentage of sales) x 100
- Overtime as a % of labour cost
- Operating profit margin % by month

3.2 **(a)** The customers are key stakeholders. The product is very specialised and there are few businesses who supply these products. This is evidenced by the repeat business and long-term nature of the customer relationships.

The customers are likely to want to see the financial statements, to allow them to analyse Almost Vintage Limited's liquidity and gearing, to ensure they will continue to trade and supply them. They may also investigate the gross margin, when considering future pricing.

The suppliers are key stakeholders .They want Almost Vintage Limited to continue to trade so the suppliers can continue to sell to them.

The suppliers will want to see the financial statements to determine how much credit they should give Almost Vintage Limited.

The owner Narita is a key stakeholder. She will want to know how the business is performing and how profitable it is so she can take money out in the form of salary and dividends.

(b) The key performance indicators the owner will want to review include:

- Gross profit margin % by product
- Operating profit margin %
- Weekly/monthly sales figures
- Trade receivable days
- Trade payable days
- Labour cost %
- Wastage % (material wasted/ total material purchased)
- Overtime % (overtime payments/ total wages)

3.3

Ratio	Formulae	Calculation
Gross profit percentage	Gross profit / Revenue x 100(%)	15,200 / 36,000 x 100 = 42.2%
Operating profit percentage	Operating profit / Revenue x 100(%)	13,310 / 36,000 x 100 = 37.0%
Return on shareholders' funds	Profit after tax / Total equity x 100(%)	866 / 26,950 x 100 = 3.2%
Current ratio	Current assets / current liabilities	7,453 / 2,711 = 2.7 : 1
Acid test / Quick ratio	Current assets – Inventories / Current liabilities	7,453 – 2,736 / 2,711 = 1.7 : 1
Gearing	Non-current liabilities / Total equity + Non-current liabilities x 100(%)	3,500 / (26,950 + 3,500) x 100 = 11.5%
Inventory holding period	Inventory / Cost of sales x 365	2,736 / 20,800 x 365 = 48.0 days
Trade receivable collection period	Trade receivables / revenue x 365 (days)	3,960 / 36,000 x 365 = 40.2 days
Trade payables payment period	Trade payables / Cost of Sales x 365 (days)	1,786 / 20,800 x 365 = 31.3 days

3.4 (a) Engaging in unethical behaviour

3.5 (d) Engaging in unethical behaviour

3.6 (c) Social equality

3.7 **(a)** (c) Objectivity

(b) (b) Decline politely

CHAPTER 4: INTERNAL CONTROL SYSTEMS AND FRAUD

4.1 (d) All of the above – All the directors are jointly responsible for putting in systems and controls to prevent and detect fraud.

4.2 Theft, false accounting or misrepresentation, bribery and corruption, deception.

4.3 Segregation of duties is where no one person is able to completely record a financial transaction from beginning to end.

For example, a person cannot create or raise a sales invoice, then collect and record the receipt from the customer.

This prevents fraud as it would need two or more people to hide or remove the transaction, known as collusion. Two people would need to be dishonest and work together which is less likely than an individual acting alone.

4.4 **(a)** **Theft of cash sales** – Customers order and pay for one-off items on site and Gino has no record of their 'order'. The invoice book is generic. The gardener could use a similar invoice book he has purchased and give this to the customer, as a receipt. The gardener could then take the money and Gino would not know of the sale.

Claiming additional hours not worked – The employee could submit additional hours for the maintenance work done, which was not performed. Gino pays them based on the timesheets, so additional pay would be given without question.

(b) **Theft of cash sales**

Risk of Fraud – High. As employees know there is no system for tracing back missing sales, which could be a reasonable amount at certain times of year, they could easily commit the fraud.

Impact on business – Medium. The one-off items are likely to be relatively small compared to the day-to-day contracts

Claiming additional hours not worked

Risk of fraud – High. Employees are aware there is no control over recording how long they spend doing each job.

Impact on Business – Low. Gino has knowledge of the business and knows how long it takes for each maintenance job. He would be likely to query additional hours.

(c) **Theft of cash sales** – Customers need to request additional work via email to Gino. He will then be able to match the request to an invoice and payment.

Claiming additional hours – Each customer must sign the timesheet agreeing the amount of time each gardener spends on site.

4.5 The changes in the ratios and key data and the potential weaknesses which may exist in the systems are as follows:

1. Drop in sales revenue – given there is no mention of a down turn in trade for any of the shops, it is possible that all cash sales are not being recorded properly. This would also be highlighted by the reduction in the gross profit margin from 40% to 32%, as the cost of sales would be included for the items but the revenue would not.

2. Reduction in distribution costs as a percentage of revenue – you would expect this to remain the same. It has reduced slightly and it could be that the business has incorrected recorded distribution costs in Cost of Sales, due to general ledger coding errors. This would also partly explain the change in the gross profit margin %.

3. Increase in inventory days – this year's inventory value may be recorded incorrectly at the end of the year. The process for determining the year end valuation needs to be investigated. If it is an inventory count at the year end, the inventory should be re-examined to ensure obsolete items and items where net realisable value is less then cost are written down correctly. If the value is overstated, this would make the gross profit margin % even worse.

4. Trade receivable collection days are increased. This may indicate a problem with Credit Control procedures, if customers are not being chased promptly. This could also occur if the cash sales recording was inadequate, as the receivables balance would be calculated using a lower revenue figures, making it appear unusually high.

4.6 **Labour %**

The Manager is expected to authorise additional hours for the part-time employee to work past 1.00pm when the shop is busy. As the labour percentage is 10% higher for this period than last period, but the sales value per day is lower, this does not appear to have been happening. Alternatively, there may be a problem with the wage rates being paid to staff or an issue in recording of revenue, which makes sales lower, so the labour percentage is higher.

Value of waste bread %

This appears to be very high, especially as sales value per day is low. The waste has more than doubled. This will, in part, be due to the reduced sales value. The bakers may have stopped reviewing sales levels and producing the correct products that are selling well. If this is not being done and sales are lower, then wastage will inevitably be higher.

There could be an issue with the valuing of wastage this period compared to last if the Manager changed what she does. There may be cakes or bread being thrown away unnecessarily or staff could be taking some bread and cakes home and recording it as wastage.

Average sales value per day

The sales made each day will vary but should smooth out over the course of four weeks. If the bakers have stopped reviewing what is selling well, the customers may not be able to buy the goods they want, so sales will be lower.

Nina should review the takings by day to see if there is a pattern to the reduced sales. If sales were lower on Saturdays, for example, she may wish to monitor the takings and till more closely, as a member of staff could be taking money from the till. She should ensure the sales information ties back to the banking and it is not an error simply in how the money is entered into the till and records.

4.7

Details of Risk	Employees	Collusion	Likelihood	Impact & Grade (5-1)	Possible control
IT Theft of customer pricing due to open access to files	Accounts, IT	None	High	High 5	Authorised access only to customer pricing files, password protected
Payroll Wages payments overstated on timesheets	Production hourly paid	None	High	Medium 3	Supervisor to authorise timesheets
Warehouse Taking inventory for own use or selling on	Stores, Production	Third party recipients	Moderate	Medium 3	Warehouse and stores locked and movements controlled in and out. Regular inventory record to physical counts and differences investigated

CHAPTER 5: EFFECTIVE ACCOUNTING SYSTEMS

5.1 (b) Two*Nine-7 – This has a mixture of letters, lower and upper case, numbers and other symbols.

5.2 No, the Purchase Ledger Clerk is not correct. The purchase ledger control account reconciliation reconciles the list of suppliers' balances with the summary postings on the general ledger.

Errors the reconciliation will find include:

- purchase invoices debited to supplier's accounts
- sales invoices posted to the accounts payable control account

Errors the reconciliation would not find include:

- a pricing error in a purchase invoice
- a purchase invoice posted to the wrong supplier account
- VAT in a purchase invoice posted to rent instead of VAT control
- missing credit notes
- missing purchase invoices

5.3 Refer to pages 95 to 97 for examples

5.4

Email

To: S. Addle, Managing Director, Pedal for Miles Limited

From: S. Poak, Accountant

Subject: Proposed payroll system

Further to our recent conversation regarding the increasing fees of the payroll bureau, I set out below the main areas we would need to undertake, should we decide to bring the payroll in-house.

Data collection and storage

- The timesheet system we currently have in place for production staff will continue to be used as the basis for the recording of hours worked. These are currently approved by the Supervisor.
- Salaried staff are paid monthly, based on their contracts.
- Additional payments, eg bonuses or commission will continue to be authorised by the appropriate Director on the 'Variation forms' we currently use for the bureau.
- We will need to enter into a payroll system and keep securely details of the following for each person:
  - Staff number
  - Rate of pay
  - Tax code
  - National Insurance (NI) number
  - Deductions such as pension contributions, subscriptions, court orders
  - Bank details

Processing payroll

- A payroll software package will use the above data to calculate:
  - Gross pay
  - Deductions
  - Net pay
  - Gross taxable pay to date
  - Tax paid to date
- A payments list will be generated and a BACS payment file created for authorisation
- The Payroll will then need to be approved by myself
- The BACS payment will require authorisation by two signatories, then sent to the bank
- The software will generate and submit RTI, as required by HMRC
- Payslips will be generated and can be either emailed or posted

Obviously, we hold most of the data needed now, which is keep securely locked, due to its confidential data.

The next step would be to investigate payroll systems and potential staff costs. Please let me know if you wish me to proceed with this.

Best wishes

Andrea

5.5 Purchasing capital expenditure

- Capital expenditure plan produced for 5 or more years, in detail for the next year
- Board of Directors approve Capital expenditure plan
- Tendering process using approved suppliers
- Purchase order will be authorised by senior management, in line with approved budget

Managing the asset register

- Assets are barcoded and securely stored
- Ownership records are stored securely
- Regular matching of assets register to physical assets and vice versa and differences investigated
- Disposals are authorised by senior management
- Regular reconciliation of asset register to general ledger for cost, depreciation and carrying value

5.6 An effective costing system will prevent the company costing jobs incorrectly producing a quotation which gives too low a price and will lower the profitability of the company. It will prevent materials being ordered unnecessarily for jobs.

It will prevent errors and fraud in the inventory system, such as inventory being stolen or recorded incorrectly. The inventory count will prevent the records being incorrect.

The system will prevent labour and materials costs being recorded against the wrong job and for the wrong value. It will prevent excessive wastage or labour inefficiency occurring for a long period of time, as variances will be investigated. It will prevent under or over-absorption of overheads, as overheads will be monitored and adjusted when needed.

The system will prevent under or overvaluation of inventory and cost of sales in the general ledger.

CHAPTER 6: EVALUATION AND REVIEW OF AN ACCOUNTING SYSTEM

6.1

Weakness	Potential problems
There is no authorisation process over hours worked on timesheets.	Employees could be paid for hours they have not worked in error. Potential fraud – employees could add on extra hours not worked.
There does not appear to be authorisation of new starters.	Potential fraud by Branch Manager – set up of fictitious employee.
There is no independent authorisation process when an employee leaves.	The Branch Manager could delay sending the Leaver form and collude with the employee to keep the wages, as they will continue to be paid.
Timesheets are not checked for arithmetical accuracy.	Employees could be paid for hours not worked.
The cash request is only authorised by the Assistant Accountant, based on a payroll produced by the Payroll Clerk with no additional supporting information. There is no evidence of authorisation.	The Assistant Accountant or the Payroll Clerk could fraudulently request additional cash.
The wage packets are put together by the Payroll Clerk alone.	Potential fraud – wages stolen by Payroll Clerk and hidden as an error.
The cash wages are given to the Branch Manager.	Potential theft of wages by Branch Manager.
Wages are held insecurely overnight by the Branch Manager.	Potential theft and potential fraud through theft by collusion with third party.
Branch Managers pay out wages alone.	Potential theft of wages by Branch Manager.
There is no authorisation and review of the monthly payroll.	Potential for fraud or errors in payments by the Payroll Clerk. Leavers may continue to be paid if they have not been correctly processed.

6.2

Weakness	**Potential problems**
The Maintenance depot Manager can authorise and raise an order for the purchase of a new coach.	Coaches may be ordered unnecessarily. Significant expenditure may be incurred where there is no business need.
No tender process exists for purchasing coaches.	Coaches may not be competitively priced and the business may incur unnecessary additional cost. Purchases may not be supporting sustainable practices, such as low emission vehicles.
No Board level authorisation of capital expenditure.	The business may be buying assets unnecessarily.
The discount is fixed at 5% of list price as the supplier is a friend of the Managing Director.	The business may not be achieving the best possible price for capital items and be overpaying for them.
Proof of delivery is given prior to goods being inspected and passed as fit for use.	Coaches may be received and paid for, when they cannot be used by the business.
Only one person authorised the BACS payment	Possible fraud or error for the payment. Money could be paid unnecessarily.
Maintenance Depot Manager ordered and authorises payment for coaches (by sending the signed GRN).	Potential fraud through collusion with supplier to inflate price and take the difference.
Maintenance Depot Manager authorises disposal price for old coaches and informs accounts of buyer details.	Coaches could be sold at below market value. Possible fraud via collusion with purchaser of coach.
No reconciliation of physical coaches to asset register, using serial numbers.	Potential error as disposed coaches could be included incorrectly in the non-current assets register.

6.3 (a)

Strengths	**Benefits to the business**
Internet site linked to inventory and sales ordering module.	Existing customers can easily place orders online for items that are in inventory. The system will automatically check they are within credit limit, so the risk of a bad debt is reduced. The simplicity of the process makes it very quick for the customer to place orders and as the inventory is 'real time' they know the goods are produced ready to be delivered.
Promotion of products by customised email	The customers will receive promotions in line with their previous purchasing patterns, so they are more likely to buy. The promotion is a cheap way of sending them information to entice them to purchase more items. As 70% are repeat customers they are likely to buy.

(b)

Weaknesses	**Damage to the business**
The procedures for giving credit terms to new customers are inadequate, as are the credit control procedures for late payers.	By only using references to determine a credit limit, the business could be exposed unnecessarily to customers who have a poor credit history, as they are likely to send the best possible supplier references. No initial analysis of financial accounts further increases this risk. The credit controls procedures are not strong enough to ensure bad debts are minimised.
The procedures over the pricing of product are not sufficiently up to date to ensure all costs will be covered in the calculated price. The overhead absorption rates are out of date, so could be too low or too high and the materials costs are based on older prices, not current materials prices, as this is how FIFO values issues of material to production.	The pricing procedures could result in costs which are either too low or too high. Where costs are too low, the price generated may not be enough to ensure the business remains profitable. If the resulting costs are too high, the resulting price could be uncompetitive and cost the business sales.

CHAPTER 7: RECOMMENDATIONS AND MAKING CHANGES

7.1 Strength

Hotels and flights are paid for by Travel America after the customer has either paid the deposit or the final balance on the booking. The business will not make payments to suppliers unnecessarily.

As dollars are purchased for the year at an exchange rate fixed in advance, the business will be unaffected by changes in exchange rates when they pay for the hotels, trips and other expenses in dollars.

Weakness

The airline payments system does not go back and update the costs within the individual booking. There is no reconciliation between the cost of sales flight figure and the final amounts paid. Potentially, where costs are incorrect in the Reservations System, we could be undercharging the customer and losing profit. Where differences occur between payment and cost, reconciliation should be made and differences investigated, as airlines could be charging the wrong fares to Travel America.

Opportunity

The review by the Manager of booking could be used to review whether any additional sales could be made to the customer. As they are likely to know the products very well, they could see if there is any opportunity for selling more expensive or additional tours.

Threat

Our customers want to experience unique and exciting experiences. We need to work closely with our suppliers to ensure the customers have the best experiences possible. If the customers do not have good service they may chose to book with other agents or decide to book independently. We must protect our business and continue to identify innovative and unique experiences to offer to these customers.

For weaknesses, you could also have there are no supplier payment reconciliations being undertaken for hotels. Hotel costs could be incorrectly stated or missed

7.2

- The internet site could be improved to interact with inventory, not simply be an online catalogue. This would reduce the need for Sales to confirm order details and prices and so save time. It would also improve the customer service.
- Sales discounts should be authorised by a senior member of staff eg the Sales Director. This would avoid the possibility of sales staff colluding with customers to give them large discounts and receive part of the savings. Sales discounts would be minimised, maintaining the profitability of the business.
- There should be a clear procedure to identify 'one-off' customers who pay by bank transfer or PayPal have paid for the goods prior to them being despatched. The order should be marked as 'cash paid'. It should only be sent to the Warehouse once this has been done. All orders for credit customer should clearly state they are a credit customer on the order. This will avoid any accidental despatch of goods prior to payment being received. This will limit the likelihood of a bad debt in the business.
- The Despatch Note should be matched to the order and the goods compared to both prior to being sent out to the customer. The Warehouse staff should sign this as evidence of the review. This will avoid despatching the wrong goods to a customer, as the goods could be costly to get back.
- Signed proof of delivery should be kept with the order in the accounts department, so any customer queries can be easily resolved.

7.3 (a)

Weakness	Potential problem	Recommendation
The clocking in system is open to abuse, as the Manager is not present when staff clock in or clock out.	Staff could clock each other in or out, giving them extra hours worked. The staff could be paid for hours not worked.	A member of management should be present as staff clock in and clock out to ensure they are not claiming additional hours incorrectly.
Each Hotel manager has the authority to advertise for and employ staff with no other authorisation.	Staff could be hired unnecessarily. Fictitious employees could be put onto the payroll.	The Area Manager should authorise all adverts and New Starters. All new staff need to sign the New Starter Form. This will remove the threat of fraud and avoid staff being employed unnecessarily.
The Hotel Manager is able to complete all the paperwork for a new starter.	A new starter could be fictitiously added to the payroll.	The Area Manager should meet and authorise new staff.
The hotel employs many casual staff on zero hours contracts, who are from out of the area. There is a high staff turnover.	The staff may not be motivated to provide good customer service. They may be unable to earn enough to live comfortably.	The hotel should review staffing levels and consider offering contracts for people in the local area for 35 hours per week on three month basis to cover the Summer period. The customer service would be improved and overtime would be minimised. This would support sustainable practices.
The clocking in system is not linked to the payroll system. Hours and overtime are entered manually by the Payroll Clerk.	Errors could occur in the input of hours and overtime. The process is very inefficient.	Integrate the clocking in system to the Payroll system. The Payroll Clerk can undertake other duties with the time saved. Errors will not occur in the hours recorded for payment.
The BACS payment is authorised by the Financial Controller, using just the BACS payment list.	The Payroll Clerk could enter staff on the payroll fictitiously and commit fraud. Potential fraud risk.	Two people, including a Director, should authorise the BACS payment, with the payroll reports as supporting documentation.

(b) Cost Benefit Analysis

Savings:

Payroll Clerk's time 3 hrs x £15	£45.00 per week
Employer costs (NI, pension 15%)	£6.75 per week
Total saving	£51.75 per week
Total saving per year	£2,691.00
Costs	
Software costs	£500.00
Net saving	**£2,191 per year**

Other non-quantifiable benefits

– Savings made from hours incorrectly paid in prior months

– More motivated Payroll Clerk

– Ability of the Payroll Clerk to support the Accounts Team

(c) Problem

The clocking in system hours could be incorrectly loaded into the payroll system. The company could pay staff for hours or overtime they have not worked.

The Payroll Clerk may not be adequately trained to ensure the data transfer happens properly.

Controls to put in place

The Payroll Clerk will need to be trained in the new procedures.

The software should be tested for a period of time using test staff data, to ensure it is working correctly.

When the system goes 'live' the Financial Controller and the Payroll Clerk will need to reconcile all the data line by line, to ensure it has transferred over correctly, including the basic and overtime split. This process should be repeated for at least four weeks, in case any anomalies occur.

The Financial Controller should set up exception reports to identify where employees are paid significantly more or less than the previous payroll and investigate them.

Index

for your notes

for your notes

for your notes

for your notes

for your notes

for your notes

for your notes

for your notes

for your notes

for your notes